TREASURY OF LITERATURE

INTEGRATED SPELLING

GRADE 4

D1358526

HARCOURT BRACE & COMPANY

Orlando Atlanta Austin Boston San Francisco Chicago Dallas New York
Toronto London

Printed in the United States of America

ISBN 0-15-302071-7

1 2 3 4 5 6 7 8 9 10 082 97 96 95 94

Contents

MAKING

YOUR

Spelling Log

This book gives you a place to keep a word list of your own. It's called a Spelling Log!

If you need some ideas for creating your list, just look at what my friends are doing!

While I read, I look for words that I think are interesting.

I listen for new words used by other people on radio and television.

"...and now that brand new most monotonous song."

I will include words that I need to use when I write, especially words that are hard for me to spell.

Before I put a word in my log, I check the spelling. I look up the word in a dictionary or a thesaurus, or I ask a classmate for help.

CANINE?

To help me understand and remember the meaning of a word, I write a definition, a synonym, or an antonym. I also use the word in a sentence.

Here's how to use it!

The Spelling Log section of this book is just for you. It's your own list of words that you want to remember.

Your Spelling Log has three parts. Here's how to use each part.

This handy list makes it easy for me to study the words I need to learn!

Words to **Study**

This is where you'll list words from each lesson that you need to study. Include words you misspell on the pretest and any other words you aren't sure you can always spell correctly.

EMERALD FOREST • Harcourt Brace School Publishers

I'll write a clue beside each word to help me remember it.

Words to Explore

These pages are for listing the Words to Explore from each lesson in your spelling book. Group the words any way you like, and write them on the pages where you think they belong. You'll find pages for language, social studies, math and science, and art and music.

Hints in the margins may help you think of categories for your words!

Have fun!

MY OWN WORD COLLECTION

You choose the words to list on these pages. Include new words, words that are especially interesting, and any other words you want to remember. You decide how to group them, too!

Study Steps to Learn a Word

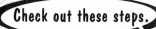

Check out these steps.

SAY THE WORD.

REMEMBER WHEN YOU HAVE HEARD THE WORD USED. THINK ABOUT WHAT IT MEANS.

LOOK AT THE WORD.

FIND ANY PREFIXES, SUFFIXES, OR OTHER WORD PARTS YOU KNOW. THINK OF ANOTHER WORD THAT IS RELATED IN MEANING AND SPELLING. TRY TO PICTURE THE WORD IN YOUR MIND.

EMERALD FOREST • Harcourt Brace School Publishers

SPELL THE WORD TO YOURSELF.

THINK ABOUT THE WAY EACH SOUND IS SPELLED. NOTICE ANY UNUSUAL SPELLING.

WRITE THE WORD WHILE YOU ARE LOOKING AT IT.

CHECK THE WAY YOU HAVE FORMED YOUR LETTERS. IF YOU HAVE NOT WRITTEN THE WORD CLEARLY OR CORRECTLY, WRITE IT AGAIN.

CHECK WHAT YOU HAVE LEARNED.

COVER THE WORD AND WRITE IT. IF YOU HAVE NOT SPELLED THE WORD CORRECTLY, PRACTICE THESE STEPS UNTIL YOU CAN WRITE IT CORRECTLY EVERY TIME.

Spelling WORDS

1. stay
2. glad
3. state
4. great
5. mail
6. plan
7. place
8. class
9. grade
10. gray
11. swam
12. stand
13. space
14. thank
15. plant
16. catch

YOUR OWN WORDS

Look for other long *a* and short *a* words to add to the lists. You might use *brave* or *strain* when writing about an athlete. You might find *track* or *balance* in a book about sports.

17. _____
18. _____
19. _____
20. _____

Words with Long and Short *a*

Each Spelling Word has the long *a* or the short *a* sound. Look at the letters that spell those sounds.

Sort the Spelling Words in a way that will help you remember them. Two example words are given.

/ā/
name

/a/
hand

The long *a* sound can be spelled *ay, a_e, ea,* or *ai.*

The short *a* sound is usually spelled *a.*

EMERALD FOREST "Mirette on the High Wire" • Harcourt Brace School Publishers

Integrated Spelling

STRATEGY Workshop

SPELLING CLUES: Rhyming Words Writers use words that rhyme to help them spell better. To help you spell a word, think of another word you know that rhymes with it. Look for spelling patterns.

Read each word below. Write a Spelling Word that rhymes with it.

1. pail   2. pass   3. bank   4. ant   5. made

6–9. Complete each sentence in the letter with a Spelling Word that rhymes with the word in parentheses.

1. _____

2. _____

3. _____

4. _____

5. _____

Dear Amanda,
    At the county circus, my __6__ (fan) is to walk on the high wire. I must __7__ (hand) on the wire very carefully. A net below will __8__ (match) me if I fall. I am __9__ (pad) that you can come!
                                    Love,
                                    Daisy

6. _____

7. _____

8. _____

9. _____

WORKING WITH MEANING Write Spelling Words to replace 10–16.

We can't __10__ here.
Why not? I feel __11__ !
Those __12__ clouds will bring rain soon.
They're at least a __13__ away!
And you're in outer __14__ !
I'm not leaving this __15__ .
The last person who told me that __16__ away!

10. _____

11. _____

12. _____

13. _____

14. _____

15. _____

16. _____

Words to Explore

acrobats

agent

balanced

wavering

Think about how you might use these words in your writing. You might list *balanced* and *wavering* in your Spelling Log under Vivid Verbs. How might you use them if you were writing about a sports event?

1. _____

2. _____

3. _____

4. _____

5. _____

_____

_____

_____

6. _____

_____

7. _____

_____

8. _____

_____

VOCABULARY WordShop

PERFORMERS Use the clues below and the words in the box to help you identify the performers in the center ring. Use a dictionary if you need help.

actors   acrobats   mimes   jugglers

1. Which performers tell stories without speaking?
2. Who shouldn't drop anything while performing?
3. Who might flip for an audience?
4. Which performers might forget their lines?
5. Write a complete sentence about one of these performers.

Add performer words to each column.

6. Television	7. Sports	8. Music
_____	_____	_____
_____	_____	_____

EMERALD FOREST "Mirette on the High Wire" • Harcourt Brace School Publishers

Integrated Spelling

What's in a Word?

Gray comes from the Old English word *græg*. In England, the correct spelling is *grey*. In the United States, *gray* is the preferred spelling, but *grey* is also acceptable.

1. Write a rhyme that includes the word *gray*.

IDIOMS Read the clues in the juggling balls. Then read each sentence. Write the clue that means the same as the underlined idiom.

2. My <u>gray matter</u> tells me the high wire is dangerous.
3. The ringmaster gave me <u>the green light</u> to try it.
4. He is a wonderful man with a <u>heart of gold</u>.
5. A chance like that comes along <u>once in a blue moon</u>.

1. _____

   _____

   _____

   _____

2. _____
3. _____
4. _____
5. _____

RHYME TIME Create rhymes with a partner. Write a Spelling Word on a sheet of paper. Pass the paper to your partner, who writes a word that rhymes with the Spelling Word. When you have added as many rhyming words as you can, begin again with another Spelling Word. After you have made five rhyming lists, choose one list. Together, write a poem using the words on that list.

Integrated Spelling

EMERALD FOREST "Mirette on the High Wire" • Harcourt Brace School Publishers

Words with Long and Short e

Each Spelling Word has the long *e* or the short *e* sound. Look at the letters that spell those sounds.

Sort the Spelling Words in a way that will help you remember them. Two example words are given.

Spelling WORDS

1. step
2. mean
3. free
4. nest
5. smell
6. speak
7. wheel
8. next
9. street
10. least
11. else
12. check
13. beach
14. teeth
15. slept
16. guess

YOUR OWN WORDS

Where might you read about a *shell* in the *sea* or other creature habitats? In that same source, look for other long and short *e* words. You also might see *web* or *leaf* in a science book.

17. _____
18. _____
19. _____
20. _____

/ē/
eat

/e/
bed

The long *e* sound can be spelled *ea* or *ee*.

The short *e* sound is usually spelled *e*.

EMERALD FOREST "Finding the Green Stone" • Harcourt Brace School Publishers

Integrated Spelling

Name _____

STRATEGY Workshop

SPELLING CLUES: Comparing Spellings Think about ways the long *e* and the short *e* sounds may be spelled. Look for spelling patterns. Try different spellings until each word looks correct.

Think about the vowel sound, and write the spelling that looks correct.

1. whel   wheel
2. step   steap
3. else   eals
4. sleeped   slept
5. cheak   check
6. least   lest

1. _____
2. _____
3. _____
4. _____
5. _____
6. _____

7–11. Complete the journal entry. Think about the vowel sound, and write the correct spelling.

May 22

Today, I found a bird's
__7__ (nest/nast) in our
cherry tree. A baby bird had fallen
to the __8__ (streat/street) below, and
I saved it from our __9__ (mean/meen)
cat, which has very sharp
__10__ (teath/teeth). Soon, I
hope to set it __11__ (freal/free).

7. _____
8. _____
9. _____
10. _____
11. _____

FUN WITH WORDS Write a Spelling Word to answer each riddle with a rhyme.

Example: What do you call a tire sale? a <u>wheel</u> deal

12. What do you call the book after this one? the _____ text
13. Where do you find fruity sand? at the peach _____
14. What do you call a great odor? a swell _____
15. What do you call a clueless treasure hunt? a _____ mess
16. What do you call a hiccup? a _____ squeak

12. _____
13. _____
14. _____
15. _____
16. _____

Words to Explore

behavior

memory

radiance

realize

Think about how you might use these words in your writing. You might list *behavior* and *memory* in your Spelling Log under Characteristics. How might you use them if you were writing in a journal?

1. _____

2. _____

3. _____

4. _____

5. _____

6. _____

7. _____

8. _____

VOCABULARY WordShop

CHARACTERISTICS OF LIGHT Light can be described in many different ways. Write the word in the box that best describes each picture. Use the clues below to help you. Use a dictionary if you need help.

| radiance | iridescent | glowing | glistening |

1

2

3

4

1. The firefly sends forth a bright, fireless light.
2. The dragonfly reflects a rainbow of color.
3. This word comes from the Latin word *radius,* meaning "beam."
4. This word means "sparkling."

Complete the chart with your own words about light.

Sources of Light ⇨	What They Do
sun	⇨ shine
diamond	⇨ sparkle
5. _____	⇨ 6. _____
7. _____	⇨ 8. _____

EMERALD FOREST "Finding the Green Stone" • Harcourt Brace School Publishers

Name _____

CONTEXT CLUES Finish the comparison in each sentence.
Use one of the words in the box. If you want to know more
about the words, look them up in a dictionary.

1. My sister's doll had lips as red as _____.
2. The _____ on her costume flashed like green fire.
3. Tiny blue _____ glittered in her rings.
4. The doll's china face was as cold and hard as _____.

What's in a Word?

The French word for *teeth* is *dents*. Our name for the common yellow flower, *dandelion*,
comes from the French *dent de lion,* meaning "tooth of the lion." The leaves of the
plant have jagged edges that look like sharp, pointy teeth.

Fill in the missing letters to make three more "toothy" words
that have French or Latin roots. Write the whole word.

5. <u>d</u> <u>e</u> <u>n</u> <u>t</u> __ __ __   someone who fixes teeth

6. __ __ <u>d</u> <u>e</u> <u>n</u> <u>t</u>   a group of animals that includes
   mice, rats, and beavers

7. __ __ __ <u>d</u> <u>e</u> <u>n</u> <u>t</u>   a three-pronged spear like
   Neptune's

1. _____

2. _____

3. _____

4. _____

5. _____

6. _____

7. _____

1. sing
2. mind
3. dried
4. mine
5. trip
6. gift
7. eye
8. type
9. bring
10. wild
11. fried
12. trick
13. fifth
14. quite
15. sixth
16. spring

YOUR OWN WORDS

Look for other long *i* and short *i* words to add to the lists. You might find *inspire* or *district* in a social studies book. You might use *crisis* or *citizen* in a report on a president.

17. _____
18. _____
19. _____
20. _____

Words with Long and Short *i*

Each Spelling Word has the long *i* or the short *i* sound. Look at the letters that spell those sounds.

Sort the Spelling Words in a way that will help you remember them. Two example words are given.

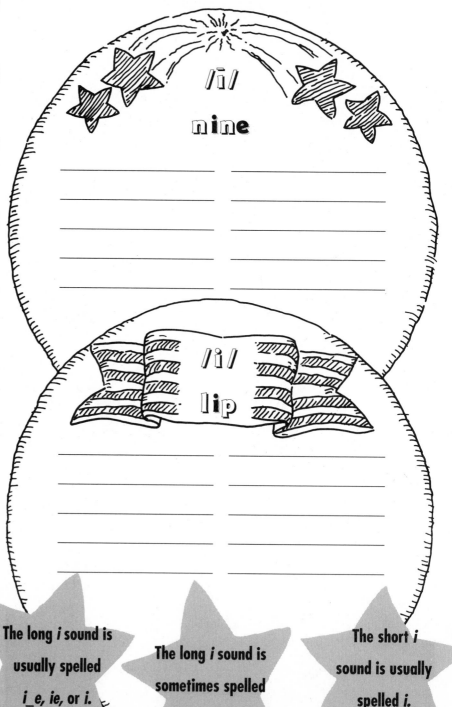

/ī/
nine

_____ _____
_____ _____
_____ _____

/ĭ/
lip

_____
_____
_____
_____

The long *i* sound is usually spelled i_e, ie, or i.

The long *i* sound is sometimes spelled y_e or eye.

The short *i* sound is usually spelled i.

Integrated Spelling

STRATEGY Workshop

PROOFREADING: Using a Dictionary If you are not sure you have spelled a word correctly, check a dictionary. The two words at the top of every dictionary page are *guide words.* Guide words tell you which words are on that page. The guide words are the first and last entry words on each page.

| wild | type | trick | quite | spring | sixth |

1–2. If the words in the box were the only words on one page of your dictionary, what would the two guide words be?

3–6. Find the Spelling Words in the box that would be found on a page with the guide words *site* and *typical.* Write those words in alphabetical order.

1. _____

2. _____

3. _____

4. _____

5. _____

6. _____

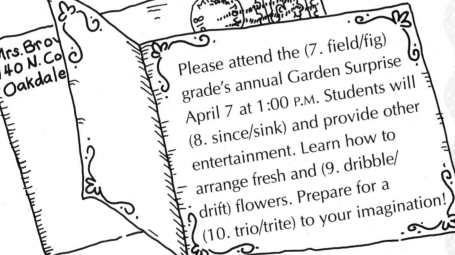

Mrs. Bro▢
140 N. Co▢
Oakdale▢

Please attend the (7. field/fig) grade's annual Garden Surprise April 7 at 1:00 P.M. Students will (8. since/sink) and provide other entertainment. Learn how to arrange fresh and (9. dribble/drift) flowers. Prepare for a (10. trio/trite) to your imagination!

7. _____

8. _____

9. _____

10. _____

7–10. Read the invitation. Use a dictionary to help you find the Spelling Word that should replace each pair of guide words. Then write the Spelling Word.

WORKING WITH MEANING Write the best Spelling Word for each definition.

11. to arrive with an item
12. cooked in oil
13. belonging to me
14. to obey
15. special present
16. organ of sight

11. _____

12. _____

13. _____

14. _____

15. _____

16. _____

Integrated Spelling

Words to Explore

admission

campaign

candidate

qualities

Think about how you might use these words in your writing. You might list *candidate* and *campaign* in your Spelling Log under Election Words. How might you use them if you were writing a speech?

1. _____

2. _____

3. _____

4. _____

5. _____

_____

_____

VOCABULARY WordShop

ELECTION WORDS An election is the process by which we choose our leaders. Use the words in the box and the clues below to help you complete the poster.

| elect | campaign | president | candidate |

Town Meeting, August 16, 7:00 P.M., Town Hall. Please attend! Think of a person you would like to nominate as a __1__ for the office of __2__. We need volunteers to organize activities for the __3__. We will __4__ a leader in November.

1. This word has the smaller word *date* in it.
2. This word is spelled almost the same way in Spanish, *presidente*.
3. This word has a silent *g* near the end.
4. This is an action word.
5. Now write three words that name qualities needed in a good leader.

What's in a Word?

Candidate comes from the Latin word *candidatus*, which means "clothed in white." Romans seeking high office wore loose white robes.

6. Find another election word. Use a reference source to learn its word history.

6. _____

_____

_____

_____

ANTONYMS The words on the campaign buttons all have opposites in the sentences below. Complete each sentence with the opposite, or antonym, of the underlined word.

1. In an election, one candidate experiences a <u>defeat</u> while the other celebrates a _____.

2. Our candidate should be a _____, not a <u>follower</u>.

3. Voters have to decide to <u>accept</u> one candidate and _____ the other.

4. The winner received the <u>majority</u> of votes; the loser received the _____.

1. _____

2. _____

3. _____

4. _____

VOWEL MATCH Write each Spelling Word on an index card. Mix up the cards, and place them face down. Play a matching game with a classmate. Take turns turning over two cards at a time. See if you can match two words with long *i* or two words with short *i*. If you make a match, take the cards. If you do not make a match, turn the cards face down again. The player with more cards at the end wins.

EMERALD FOREST "Class President" • Harcourt Brace School Publishers

Words with Long and Short *u*

1. *shut*
2. *few*
3. *crew*
4. *luck*
5. *dust*
6. *chew*
7. *hung*
8. *brush*
9. *knew*
10. *stuck*
11. *stuff*
12. *stew*
13. *bunch*
14. *truck*
15. *threw*
16. *swung*

Each Spelling Word has the long *u* or the short *u* sound. Look at the letters that spell those sounds.

Sort the Spelling Words in a way that will help you remember them. Two example words are given.

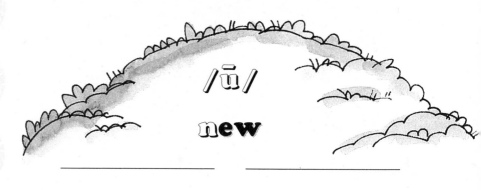

/ū/

new

_____   _____
_____   _____
_____   _____
_____

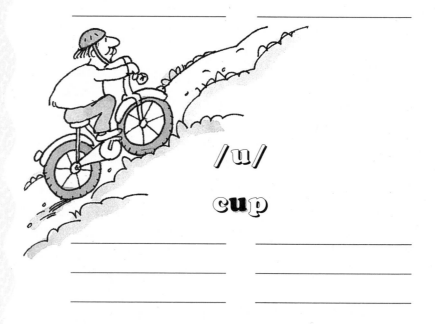

/u/

cup

_____   _____
_____   _____
_____   _____
_____   _____
_____   _____

The long *u* sound can be spelled *ew*.

The short *u* sound is usually spelled *u*.

(**YOUR OWN WORDS**)

Look for other long *u* and short *u* words to add to the lists. You might find *blew* and *pump* in a book about bicycles. You might use the words *flew* and *spun* in a report about a bike race.

17. _____
18. _____
19. _____
20. _____

EMERALD FOREST "Supergrandpa" • Harcourt Brace School Publishers

Integrated Spelling

Name _____

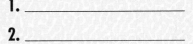

STRATEGY Workshop

SPELLING CLUES: Comparing Spellings When you're not sure how to spell a word, try writing it a few different ways. Choose the way that looks correct. Check your spelling in a dictionary.

Look at the two possible spellings. Write the spelling that looks correct.

1. swung swang   2. crue crew   3. stuw stew

4. truck trock   5. chew chue   6. brush bruch

7–10. Complete the list. Write the correct Spelling Word.

Training Reminders:
- *Buy a (7. bunch/bumch) of inner tubes.*
- *Remember to (8. shut/shot) the valves on the tires tightly.*
- *Train with a (9. few/fue) other cyclists.*
- *Carry only necessary (10. stif/stuff).*

WORKING WITH MEANING Write Spelling Words to replace 11–16.

On a bike, you don't get __11__ in traffic.

With my __12__ __13__ will fly in my face.

I __14__ a water bottle on your handlebars in case that happens.

Goggles would help, but I __15__ mine away.

I __16__ today would be perfect for a ride.

1. _____
2. _____
3. _____
4. _____
5. _____
6. _____
7. _____
8. _____
9. _____
10. _____

11. _____
12. _____
13. _____
14. _____
15. _____
16. _____

Words to Explore

cyclists
muscles
overtook
pedal

Think about how you might use these words in your writing. You might list *overtook* and *pedal* in your Spelling Log under Vivid Verbs. How might you use them if you were writing a report about a bicycle race?

1. _____
2. _____
3. _____
4. _____

5. _____
   _____
6. _____
   _____
7. _____
   _____

8. _____
9. _____

VOCABULARY WordShop

GROUPS OF PEOPLE Answer the riddles with words that name groups of people.

1. We march down the street to our own beat.
2. You can be in a big one or a small one anywhere, but you can never be alone in one.
3. Yikes! Here come racers on bikes!
4. Listening is work for us. A microphone is a big plus.

Add to the chart words that name groups of people, animals, and things.

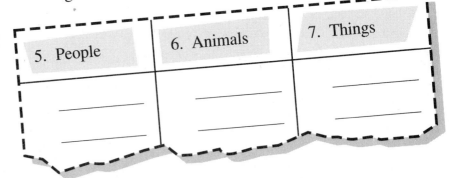

5. People	6. Animals	7. Things
_____	_____	_____
_____	_____	_____

What's in a Word?

In Sweden, a "supergrandpa" is *stalfarfar*.

8–9. Make a guess: What is the Swedish word for *grandpa*? _____ For *father*? _____

DICTIONARY: Guide Words Remember that guide words are the two words at the top of every dictionary page. Look at the guide words on each dictionary page below. Then write each word in the bike shop window on the proper dictionary page.

1. | pass   pet |
2. | reality   ripe |
3. | safety   sift |
4. | spat   sprocket |

5. Add two more words that might be entries on each dictionary page.

1. _____
2. _____
3. _____
4. _____
5. _____

_____

_____

_____

_____

_____

_____

RIDDLE IT OUT Check your knowledge of the Spelling Words for this lesson. Answer each riddle with a Spelling Word.

6. I appear like magic, but people keep wiping me out!
7. Six bananas can be this, but one cannot.
8. I bristle, but I'm not angry.
9. Five or four or three, that's me.
10. People push my pedal to the metal.

6. _____
7. _____
8. _____
9. _____
10. _____

Name _____

Practice Test

Read each sentence. Mark on the sample answer card the letter of the word that is spelled correctly and makes sense.

Example: Fran is at the _____.

A stor   B store   C stoar   D stour

1. Please _____ my letter.
   A mayl   B mall   C mail   D maile

2. I picked a _____ of flowers?
   A banch   B bunch   C bunsh   D beunch

3. Please _____ here.
   A stae   B stai   C staye   D stay

4. We have a large _____.
   A clas   B class   C clase   D cless

5. You did a _____ job.
   A great   B grate   C grait   D grayt

6. Brush your _____.
   A teath   B teth   C teeth   D teathe

7. I need at _____ a dollar.
   A leest   B least   C lest   D leist

8. Can you _____ my age?
   A ges   B geuss   C gues   D guess

9. I _____ onion soup.
   A smell   B smel   C smeal   D smeel

10. I'm learning to _____.
    A tipe   B tiep   C type   D tyep

EXAMPLE

A ● C D

ANSWERS

1 A B C D
2 A B C D
3 A B C D
4 A B C D
5 A B C D
6 A B C D
7 A B C D
8 A B C D
9 A B C D
10 A B C D

Integrated Spelling

EMERALD FOREST Unit 1 Review • Harcourt Brace School Publishers

Name _____

Read the four groups of words in each item. Find the underlined word that is spelled wrong. Mark on the sample answer card the letter for that word.

Example:

A a <u>nice</u> day B <u>pritty</u> pictures

C the fast <u>runner</u> D a long <u>movie</u>

11. A <u>fried</u> chicken B a magic <u>trick</u>

C a gold <u>myne</u> D a holiday <u>gift</u>

12. A <u>dryed</u> prunes B <u>quite</u> a person

C <u>sing</u> a song D the <u>sixth</u> of May

13. A <u>bring</u> a gift B <u>mind</u> your sister

C a <u>spring</u> day D the <u>fyfth</u> of June

14. A a long <u>trip</u> B <u>weild</u> horses

C <u>brush</u> your hair D a tree <u>trunk</u>

15. A <u>chew</u> the food B <u>hung</u> up the phone

C a <u>few</u> things D <u>throo</u> the ball

16. A <u>stuff</u> the turkey B <u>shot</u> the door

C a <u>crew</u> of sailors D mop and <u>dust</u>

17. A <u>new</u> the answer B good <u>luck</u>

C <u>swung</u> the rope D vegetable <u>stew</u>

18. A <u>round</u> wheel B got <u>stuck</u> in mud

C outer <u>spaice</u> D a <u>free</u> gift

19. A the <u>next</u> train B <u>spek</u> louder

C a <u>gray</u> horse D <u>thank</u> you

20. A across the <u>streat</u> B a big <u>step</u>

C <u>stand</u> still D a <u>place</u> to visit

EXAMPLE

Ⓐ ⬤ Ⓒ Ⓓ

ANSWERS

11 Ⓐ Ⓑ Ⓒ Ⓓ

12 Ⓐ Ⓑ Ⓒ Ⓓ

13 Ⓐ Ⓑ Ⓒ Ⓓ

14 Ⓐ Ⓑ Ⓒ Ⓓ

15 Ⓐ Ⓑ Ⓒ Ⓓ

16 Ⓐ Ⓑ Ⓒ Ⓓ

17 Ⓐ Ⓑ Ⓒ Ⓓ

18 Ⓐ Ⓑ Ⓒ Ⓓ

19 Ⓐ Ⓑ Ⓒ Ⓓ

20 Ⓐ Ⓑ Ⓒ Ⓓ

Name _____

GET THE PICTURE!

Do you want to remember a happy family celebration? Then make your own family album! Find one or more photos of your family enjoying a special occasion. It might be a birthday party or a Thanksgiving meal, for example. Tape the photos onto construction paper. Then write a paragraph that tells about the celebration. Who took part? What did everyone do? Tape your paragraph next to the photos. Give your "album" a pretty cover with your own design.

TIPS FOR SPELLING SUCCESS In your paragraph, look for places where you can combine sentences that share the same subject. Also check to see that you haven't written any run-on sentences or sentence fragments. Then check all your spelling.

IT'S YOUR HOLIDAY!!

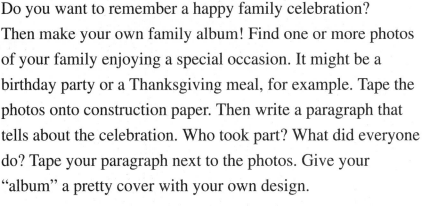

Invent a special day you'd like to celebrate. How about National Children's Day? Backward Day? Hurray for Pets Day? Write an official proclamation that announces your holiday. Give your holiday a name. Tell exactly what your new holiday celebrates. Finally, describe the many ways people can observe your holiday.

TIPS FOR SPELLING SUCCESS To make your proclamation look "official," you'll want to avoid misspelled words. Use a dictionary to check any words you are unsure of. Some words to watch for are listed on the left.

Words
to watch for
· · · · · · · · · · · · · · ·
activities
celebrate
excitement
fantastic
gifts
invitations
joyous
musical
Saturday
terrific

Name _____

GIFT BOOKS

Holiday time is just around the corner. What's the perfect gift for your family and friends? Books, of course! Make a list of the books you read this year. Choose several as gifts, and create a book cover for each book you choose. Then add some colorful ribbon as gift wrapping. Present each cover to someone who might enjoy reading that book.

TIPS FOR SPELLING SUCCESS When you write the book title and the author's name on your cover, be sure to spell them correctly. Make sure that you capitalize properly.

RHYME A RIDDLE

Here's a fun game to play with a friend. Think of a word you know how to spell, such as *state.* Tell your friend another word that rhymes with it. Your friend then tries to guess the word, making up riddles for you to answer. Here's how it works:

Then switch roles and play again with another word!

TIPS FOR SPELLING SUCCESS You might want to use a thesaurus to help you. Also, don't forget to use Study Steps to Learn a Word to help you learn to spell any words you often spell wrong.

EMERALD FOREST Unit 1 Review • Harcourt Brace School Publishers

Spelling WORDS

1. lock
2. vote
3. flow
4. odd
5. chop
6. gold
7. toes
8. plot
9. socks
10. float
11. stock
12. knocked
13. coach
14. solve
15. close
16. knowing

YOUR OWN WORDS

In what book might you read how farmers *hoe* their *crops*? In that same book, look for other long *o* and short *o* words to add to the lists. You might use *oats* or *hog* in a farm report.

17. _____
18. _____
19. _____
20. _____

Words with Long and Short *o*

Each Spelling Word has the long *o* or the short *o* sound. Look at the letters that spell those sounds.

Sort the Spelling Words in a way that will help you remember them. Two example words are given.

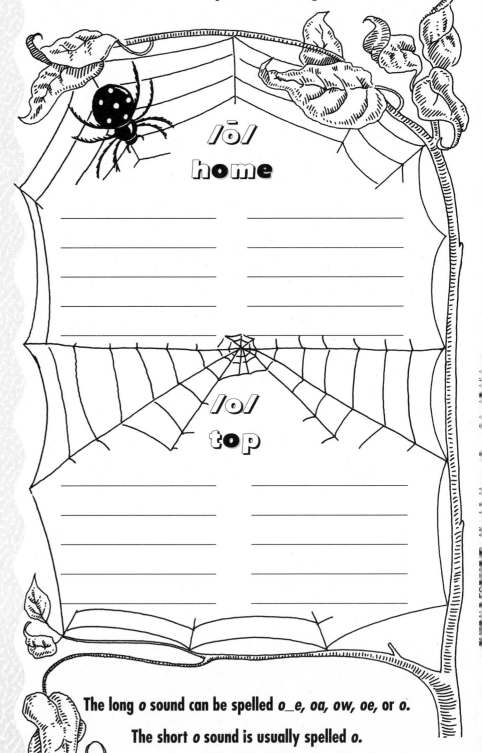

/ō/
home

/o/
top

The long *o* sound can be spelled *o_e*, *oa*, *ow*, *oe*, or *o*.

The short *o* sound is usually spelled *o*.

STRATEGY Workshop

SPELLING CLUES: Rhyming Words To help you remember how a word is spelled, study the word. Think of a rhyming word that has the same spelling pattern.

Read each word below. Write a Spelling Word that rhymes with it.

1. slow   2. hot   3. roach

4. shop   5. cold

6–9. Complete the journal entry with a Spelling Word that rhymes with the word in parentheses.

1. _____
2. _____
3. _____
4. _____
5. _____

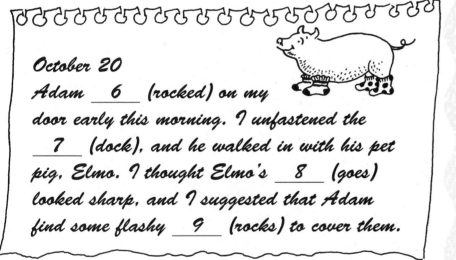

October 20
Adam __6__ (rocked) on my
door early this morning. I unfastened the
__7__ (dock), and he walked in with his pet
pig, Elmo. I thought Elmo's __8__ (goes)
looked sharp, and I suggested that Adam
find some flashy __9__ (rocks) to cover them.

6. _____
7. _____
8. _____
9. _____

WORKING WITH MEANING Write Spelling Words to replace 10–16.

It would be fun __10__ how to swim and __11__ in a pool.

But think how __12__ it might look!

Let's __13__ our eyes and dream of swimming.

I __14__ "Yes" for that!

I wish they would __15__ bathing suits for us.

That would __16__ all our problems!

10. _____
11. _____
12. _____
13. _____
14. _____
15. _____
16. _____

EMERALD FOREST "The Miracle" • Harcourt Brace School Publishers

Words to Explore

· · · · · · · · · · · · · ·

pale

delicate

ordinary

glistened

Think about how you might use these words in your writing. You might list *delicate* and *pale* in your Spelling Log under Sensory Words. How might you use them if you were writing a descriptive paragraph?

1. _____

2. _____

3. _____

4. _____

5. _____

_____

6. _____

_____

7. _____

_____

8. _____

_____

9. _____

_____

VOCABULARY WordShop

SENSORY WORDS Sensory words tell how something looks, sounds, feels, tastes, or smells. Replace the underlined words in the clues below with sensory words from the picture.

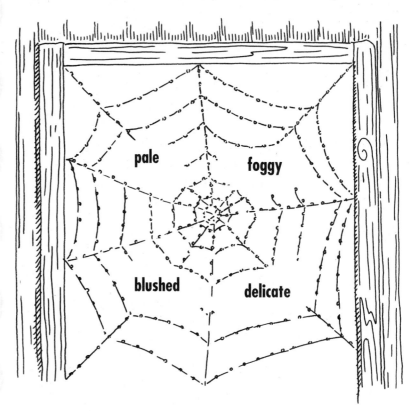

1. The sky was faintly <u>reddened</u> with dawn.
2. The farmer looked through the <u>misty</u> morning air.
3. The barn looked like a <u>nearly white</u> ghost.
4. Across the door was a <u>soft</u> spider web.

Add some sensory words of your own to the chart.

5. Sights	6. Sounds	7. Tastes	8. Smells	9. Touch
_____	_____	_____	_____	_____
_____	_____	_____	_____	_____

Name _____

What's in a Word?

Spider comes from the Old English word *spinnan*, "to spin." Spiders play important roles in many legends and folktales. In a Muskogee (Creek Indian) tale, Grandmother Spider puts the sun up in the sky. Also, many African folktales feature a crafty spider named Anansi, who often gets into trouble.

1. Write a silly title for a legend about a curious spider.

1. _____

   _____

HOMOGRAPHS The words on the web are homographs. Write the word that matches each set of clues. If you need help, use a dictionary.

2. The spider stays _____ to the web.

   Some plants _____ their leaves to trap their prey.

3. A strong _____ can damage a spider web.

   Some insects _____ up accidentally in the sticky threads.

4. It is possible to _____ a spider's web.

   If an insect were trapped, would you shed a _____?

5. It's a shame that a spider can't tie a _____.

   How would a spider _____ before a queen?

wind
bow
close
tear

2. _____

3. _____

4. _____

5. _____

GUESS-A-WORD Play a guessing game with a partner. Give one-word clues about a Spelling Word. See if your partner can guess the word. Try to use sensory words in your clues!

key
rusty
deadbolt

LOCK!!!

EMERALD FOREST "The Miracle" • Harcourt Brace School Publishers

Spelling WORDS

1. age
2. city
3. science
4. edge
5. since
6. judge
7. center
8. once
9. page
10. pencil
11. voice
12. bridge
13. gym
14. region
15. police
16. orange

YOUR OWN WORDS

Look for other words like *once* and *age* to add to the lists. You might find *sight* or *stage* in a book about the blind. You might use *race* or *jump* in a report about dogs.

17. _____
18. _____
19. _____
20. _____

Words Like *once* and *age*

Each Spelling Word has the /s/ or the /j/ sound. Look at the letters that spell those sounds.

Sort the Spelling Words in a way that will help you remember them. One example word is given. Fill in the other one as you are sorting.

/s/
ice

_____   _____
_____   _____
_____   _____
_____

/j/

_____

_____   _____
_____   _____
_____   _____
_____

The *s* sound can be spelled *c, ce, s,* or *sc.*

The *j* sound can be spelled *g, ge, dg,* or *j.*

Integrated Spelling

EMERALD FOREST "A Guide Dog Puppy Grows Up" • Harcourt Brace School Publishers

STRATEGY Workshop

PROOFREADING: Comparing Spellings When you proofread, look for words that may be misspelled. Write each word a few different ways. Then decide which spelling is correct.

Look at the two possible spellings. Write the spelling that looks correct. Use the Spelling Dictionary for help.

1. voise voice
2. bridge brije
3. senter center
4. region rejion
5. sciense science

1. _____
2. _____
3. _____
4. _____
5. _____

6–9. Proofread the letter. Four spelling errors are <u>underlined</u>. Write each word correctly.

Dear Aunt Karen,
Thank you for the pet puppy you gave me. I've wanted one <u>sinse</u> I was four. The dog is the perfect <u>aje</u> to start training. I got it an <u>oranje</u> feeding dish. A <u>polise</u> officer told me to get a dog tag, too.

Love,
Alice

6. _____
7. _____
8. _____
9. _____

WORKING WITH MEANING An analogy is a comparison of kinds of items. Write the Spelling Word that completes each analogy.

Example: *Airplane* is to *sky* as *car* is to *street*.

10. *Texas* is to *state* as *Dallas* is to _____.
11. *Read* is to *library* as *exercise* is to _____.
12. *Paint* is to *brush* as *write* is to _____.
13. *Two* is to *twice* as *one* is to _____.
14. *Team* is to *umpire* as *jury* is to _____.
15. *Wall* is to *brick* as *book* is to _____.
16. *Middle* is to *center* as *rim* is to _____.

10. _____
11. _____
12. _____
13. _____
14. _____
15. _____
16. _____

Words to Explore

instructor

kennel

graduation

campus

Think about how you might use these words in your writing. You might list *campus* and *instructor* in your Spelling Log under School Words. How might you use them if you were writing a graduation speech?

1. _____

2. _____

3. _____

4. _____

5. _____

_____

6. _____

_____

VOCABULARY WordShop

SCHOOL WORDS Some words tell about school. Complete each sentence below with a school word.

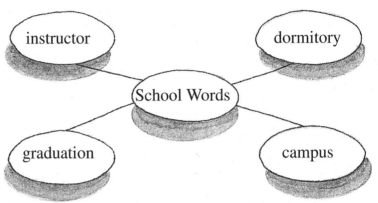

instructor

dormitory

School Words

graduation

campus

1. Ed went to college after _____ from high school.

2. The college _____ had two sports fields and ten buildings.

3. Ed lived in a _____ room with two roommates.

4. His math _____ was his favorite teacher.

5. List school words that you would add to the word web. Include people, places, actions, and things.

What's in a Word?

Gym is a shortened form of the word *gymnasium*. In the United States, a gymnasium is a room for exercising. But in Germany, a gymnasium is a high school that prepares students for college.

6. Write a conversation between a German student and an American student. Show how each person would use the word *gymnasium.*

EMERALD FOREST "A Guide Dog Puppy Grows Up" • Harcourt Brace School Publishers

Name _____

SHORTENED WORDS Each word on the doghouse has a shorter form. Write the word that matches each clue below.

1. This word refers to an afternoon meal and has been shortened to *lunch*.
2. This word refers to something people ride and has been shortened to *bus*.
3. This word's spelling changes in its shortened form, *mike*.
4. This word names an illness and has been shortened to *flu*.

5–9. Find five words you can shorten in the paragraph below. Write the words and their shortened forms.

   This is a photograph of my niece, a veterinarian. She had just passed her examination and was on her way home on her bicycle. Guess what her first patient was. A rhinoceros!

1. _____

2. _____

3. _____

4. _____

5. _____
_____

6. _____
_____

7. _____
_____

8. _____
_____

9. _____
_____

NAME THAT SOUND Read the Spelling Words to a partner. Have your partner tell you whether the *s* sound in each word is spelled *s, sc, ce,* or *c*. Ask your partner if the *j* sound is spelled *g, ge, dg,* or *j*. Next, have your partner read each word, and you name the letters that make each *s* or *j* sound.

Integrated Spelling

Spelling WORDS

1. tooth
2. into
3. hook
4. truth
5. route
6. goods
7. balloon
8. whom
9. wool
10. loose
11. student
12. wooden
13. truly
14. smooth
15. raccoon
16. through

YOUR OWN WORDS

Look for other words like *tooth* and *hook* to add to the lists. You might find *moose* or *hoof* in a book about animals. You might use *lagoon* or *woods* in a report on foxes.

17. _____
18. _____
19. _____
20. _____

Words Like *tooth* and *hook*

Each Spelling Word has the vowel sound heard in *tooth* or the vowel sound *hook*. Look at the letters that spell those sounds.

Sort the Spelling Words in a way that will help you remember them. One example word is given. Fill in the other one as you are sorting.

soon

_____   _____

_____   _____

_____   _____

_____   _____

_____   _____

_____   _____

_____

_____

_____

The vowel sound in words like *tooth* can be spelled *oo, o, u, ou,* or *ough*.

The vowel sound in words like *hook* can be spelled *oo*.

S T R A T E G Y Workshop

PROOFREADING: Checking Vowels Before writing a word, think of the different ways the vowel sound can be spelled. Choose the way that looks correct.

Add the missing vowels. Write the Spelling Words.

1. int __
2. ball __ __ n
3. thr __ __ __ __
4. r __ __ te
5. tr __ ly
6. sm __ __ th

7–11. Read the poster below. Five spelling errors are underlined. Check the vowels. Then circle each underlined word and spell it correctly.

Warning! A fox is <u>lose</u> in our area. It has already attacked a <u>raccon</u>. It was last seen near the old <u>wouden</u> bridge. The <u>trothe</u> is that the fox must be caught! Are you someone on <u>whum</u> we can count?

1. _____
2. _____
3. _____
4. _____
5. _____
6. _____

7. _____
8. _____
9. _____
10. _____
11. _____

FUN WITH WORDS Write a Spelling Word to answer each riddle with a rhyme.

12. What do you call a careful schoolchild? a prudent _____

13. What do you call a steer with sheep's skin? a _____ bull

14. What do you call items used in the forest? woods _____

15. What do you call a thief of a curved metal tool? a _____ crook

16. Where do teeth go to make a telephone call? a _____ booth

12. _____
13. _____
14. _____
15. _____
16. _____

Words to Explore

intensity
lightning
fury
cowering

Think about how you might use these words in your writing. You might list *intensity* and *lightning* in your Spelling Log under Weather Words. How might you use them if you were writing a weather report?

1. _____
2. _____
3. _____
4. _____

5. _____
_____
6. _____
_____
7. _____
_____
8. _____
_____
_____
_____

VOCABULARY WordShop

WEATHER WORDS Use the clues below to complete the Weather Bulletin.

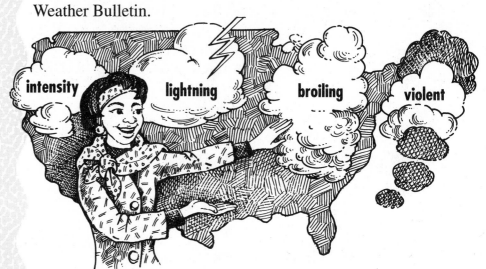

Temperatures remain in the nineties under a __1__ sun. Meanwhile, Hurricane Robert's winds are building in __2__ as it heads toward the Panhandle. As a result, __3__ storms are bringing severe __4__ and rain to Central Florida.

Add the words from the tornado to the chart. Then list as many other words related to weather as you can.

Weather

5. Kinds of Wind	6. Kinds of Storms	7. Temperature Words	8. Weather Words
___	___	___	___
___	___	___	___

EMERALD FOREST "The Midnight Fox" • Harcourt Brace School Publishers

Integrated Spelling

The word *route* is pronounced differently in different parts of the country. Some people say the word so that it rhymes with *out*. Others say the word so that it rhymes with *boot*. Both pronunciations are correct.

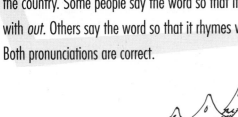

1. _____

_____

envelope
greasy
either
roof

1. Write a list of words that rhyme with *route*.

DIALECTS A *dialect* is the way language is spoken in a particular region. Each word on the fox can be pronounced two different ways, depending on the dialect. Answer the questions about the words.

2. Which word can rhyme with *easy* or *D.C.*? It refers to something slippery.

3. Which word has a syllable that rhymes with *my* or *me*? It means "one or the other."

4. Which word has a syllable that rhymes with *swan* or *pen*? It refers to something in the mail.

5. Which word has a vowel sound that is the same as the one in *goof* or the one in *foot*? It names a part of a house.

2. _____

3. _____

4. _____

5. _____

QUICK CHECK Check yourself to see how familiar you are with the Spelling Words. Add one or two vowels to each item below to make a word on the spelling list. Write each Spelling Word.

6. t ___ th
7. l ___ se
8. h ___ k
9. tr ___ ly
10. tr ___ th
11. sm ___ th
12. g ___ ds
13. thr ___ gh
14. w ___ l
15. w ___ den

6. _____

7. _____

8. _____

9. _____

10. _____

11. _____

12. _____

13. _____

14. _____

15. _____

EMERALD FOREST "The Midnight Fox" • Harcourt Brace School Publishers

Spelling WORDS

1. cent
2. hole
3. pear
4. board
5. herd
6. peace
7. planes
8. pair
9. sent
10. piece
11. whole
12. bored
13. heard
14. scent
15. plains
16. pare

YOUR OWN WORDS

Look for other homophones to add to the lists. You might find *deer* and *dear* in a book about animals. You might use *road, rowed,* and *rode* in a report on Native Americans.

17. _____
18. _____
19. _____
20. _____

Homophones

Each Spelling Word is pronounced exactly like another word but has a different spelling and meaning. Such words are called *homophones.*

Sort the Spelling Words into groups of homophones. Some groups will have two words that sound alike, and some groups will have three words that sound alike.

Two Words

_____ _____
_____ _____
_____ _____
_____ _____

Three Words

_____ _____
_____ _____
_____
_____
_____

***Homophones* are words that are pronounced the same but have different meanings and spellings.**

EMERALD FOREST "Dream Wolf" • Harcourt Brace School Publishers

S T R A T E G Y Workshop

SPELLING CLUES: Meaning When you write a homophone, make sure you spell the word so that it has the meaning that you intend.

Write the Spelling Word that matches each meaning.

1. group of cattle
2. delivered
3. flatlands
4. to cut or trim
5. piece of wood
6. flying machines

7–11. Write the Spelling Word that can replace the underlined word or words in each sentence on the note card below.

> ### Wolves
>
> A <u>pear</u> of hungry wolves hunted for food.
> One wolf found and ate a <u>pair</u>.
> Then it dug an <u>empty space</u> in the earth.
> It buried a small <u>part</u> of the fruit.
> Can a wolf detect the <u>smell</u> underground?

1. _____
2. _____
3. _____
4. _____
5. _____
6. _____

7. _____
8. _____
9. _____
10. _____
11. _____

WORKING WITH MEANING Write Spelling Words to replace 12–16.

Have you <u>12</u> the story of the big bad wolf?

That <u>13</u> story makes me angry!

I wish the kids would get <u>14</u> with hearing it.

The tale isn't worth a <u>15</u>.

Why can't people let us live in <u>16</u>?

12. _____
13. _____
14. _____
15. _____
16. _____

Words to Explore

climb

roams

twilight

wounded

Think about how you might use these words in your writing. You might list *climb* and *roams* in your Spelling Log under Vivid Verbs. How might you use them if you were writing a sports report?

1. _____

2. _____

3. _____

4. _____

5. _____

_____

_____

6. _____

_____

_____

VOCABULARY WordShop

EXACT WORDS Use the picture clues to help you choose the exact word from the box that replaces the underlined word or words in each sentence below.

climbed   trotted   crawled   roams

1. The boy <u>moved</u> up the steep rock.
2. He <u>moves</u> from place to place, no goal in mind.
3. He <u>moved on hands and knees</u> through the tiny cave.
4. A wolf <u>ran slowly</u> in front of him.

Think of ways in which people and animals move. Add your own words to the chart.

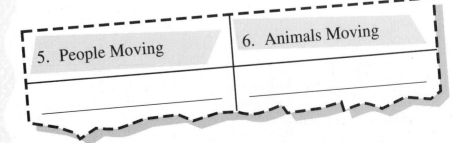

5. People Moving

6. Animals Moving

Integrated Spelling

EMERALD FOREST "Dream Wolf" • Harcourt Brace School Publishers

What's in a Word?

The word *plains* refers to an area of flatlands. The Plains Indians lived on the plains east of the Rocky Mountains. In Argentina, plains are called *pampas*. In South Africa, a plain is a *veldt*.

1. Use an encyclopedia or a thesaurus. Find one more word for *plains*.

1. _____
_____
_____

NATIVE AMERICAN WORDS The words in the Lakota shield have come from different Native American languages. Write the word that matches each clue.

toboggan
moose
moccasin
canoe
pecan
tepee

2. This Algonquian word names a soft leather slipper.
3. This Lakota word names a cone-shaped tent.
4. This Micmac word names a long, flat sled.
5. This Carib word names a long, narrow boat.
6. This is the Algonquian word for a big animal related to deer.
7. This is the Ojibwa word for a large, delicious nut.

2. _____
3. _____
4. _____
5. _____
6. _____
7. _____

HOMOPHONE HUNT With a classmate, look through a story in your anthology. Find as many homophones as you can. Write the words along with their homophone partners.

Spelling WORDS

1. card
2. story
3. share
4. hair
5. yours
6. before
7. parent
8. therefore
9. star
10. report
11. aware
12. area
13. morning
14. fair
15. court
16. stairs

Look for other vowel before r words to add to the lists. You might find *bark* or *hare* in a science book. You might use *harm* or *lair* in a report on wolves.

17. _____
18. _____
19. _____
20. _____

Words Like *card*, *fair*, and *yours*

Each Spelling Word has the vowel before *r* sound heard in *card*, *fair*, or *yours*. Look at the letters that spell those sounds.

Sort the Spelling Words in a way that will help you remember them. Two example words have been given. Fill in the last one as you are sorting.

car

_____
_____
_____

more

_____
_____
_____
_____

I love my lair.

The vowel before *r* sound in words like *card* is usually spelled *ar*.

The vowel before *r* sound in words like *yours* can be spelled *our*, *or*, or *ore*.

The vowel before *r* sound in words like *fair* can be spelled *are*, *air*, *ar*, or *ere*.

EMERALD FOREST "Running With the Pack" • Harcourt Brace School Publishers

Integrated Spelling

STRATEGY Workshop

SPELLING CLUES: Guessing and Checking When you're not sure how to spell a word, take a guess. After you try out your own spelling, check to see if you are right.

Look at the two possible spellings. Guess which is correct and circle the word. Then check and write the correct Spelling Word.

1. card corde   2. pairent parent   3. report repoart

4. awear aware   5. fair fer   6. therefore therefoar

7–10. Complete the classified ad. Write the correct spelling. If you are not sure how a word is spelled, guess and check.

> **Wildlife Adventures**
> If you have a (7. stoary/story)
> to (8. shear/share) about
> wildlife in your (9. airea/area),
> write it now! Submit it
> (10. before/befour) May 8.

1. _____
2. _____
3. _____
4. _____
5. _____
6. _____
7. _____
8. _____
9. _____
10. _____

WORKING WITH MEANING Write the Spelling Word that completes each analogy correctly.

11. *My* is to *mine* as *your* is to _____.
12. *Moon* is to *evening* as *sun* is to _____.
13. *Football* is to *stadium* as *tennis* is to _____.
14. *Ride* is to *elevator* as *walk* is to _____.
15. *Foot* is to *toes* as *head* is to _____.
16. *Ground* is to *grass* as *sky* is to _____.

11. _____
12. _____
13. _____
14. _____
15. _____
16. _____

Words to Explore

survive

prey

endangered

wilderness

Think about how you might use these words in your writing. You might list *endangered* and *survive* in your Spelling Log under Survival Words. How might you use them if you were writing a science report?

1. _____

2. _____

3. _____

4. _____

5. _____

6. _____

7. _____

8. _____

9. _____

_____

_____

VOCABULARY WordShop

CONSERVATION WORDS Some words tell about animals whose future is threatened. Complete the flowchart. Use the clues and the Words to Explore to help you.

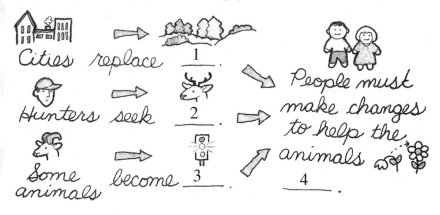

Cities replace ___1___.

Hunters seek ___2___.

Some animals become ___3___.

People must make changes to help the animals ___4___.

1. This word has the small word *wild* in it.
2. This word has an *e* that sounds like a long *a*.
3. This word has the word *danger* in it.
4. This word means "to stay alive."

Now think of words that you might use to write a report on conservation. Add them to the word web.

5. _____

Conservation Words

6. _____

7. _____

8. _____

What's in a Word?

Wilderness comes from the Middle English word *wildern*, which means "wild." *Wildern* was derived from the Old English word *wildēoren*, which means "of wild beasts" (wilde [wild] + deor [beast]).

9. Can you think of three other words that begin with the word *wild*? Write them.

DICTIONARY: Many Meanings Many words in the dictionary have more than one meaning. Each new meaning is numbered. You can use the dictionary to check whether you used the word correctly in a sentence. Read the dictionary entry below for *bound*. Write the number of the correct meaning each time the word appears in the paragraph below.

> **bound** (bound) **1.** *v.* to leap; **2.** *n.* boundary, limit; **3.** *adj.* on the way to, destined for; **4.** *v.* made fast, tied with bonds; **5.** *adj.* certain, sure.

Yesterday I was hiking, *bound* _____ for home, my purchases from town *bound* _____ up tightly in my pack. I'd just reached the stone that marks the *bounds* _____ of my large farm, when I saw a wolf cub *bound* _____ across my path. I held still and watched; the parents were *bound* _____ to be nearby.

6. Write a sentence using two different meanings of the word *bound*.

1. _____
2. _____
3. _____
4. _____
5. _____

6. _____
   _____
   _____
   _____
   _____
   _____

SILLY SENTENCES Write the beginning of a sentence, and challenge a partner to finish it. See how many Spelling Words you can use in the sentence. Make your sentences wild and silly. Try to use at least four Spelling Words in one sentence.

Name _____

Practice Test

Read each sentence. Mark the circle on the sample answer card to tell whether the underlined word is correct or incorrect.

Example: We went on a picknick.

⃝ correct ⃝ incorrect

1. The coach helped the players.

   ⃝ correct ⃝ incorrect

2. How old must you be to voat?

   ⃝ correct ⃝ incorrect

3. Ed scent a letter.

   ⃝ correct ⃝ incorrect

4. Eat a green pare.

   ⃝ correct ⃝ incorrect

5. Would you like an orange?

   ⃝ correct ⃝ incorrect

6. This brije is made of steel.

   ⃝ correct ⃝ incorrect

7. Let's blow up a ballon.

   ⃝ correct ⃝ incorrect

8. I like your wul sweater.

   ⃝ correct ⃝ incorrect

9. I worked all through the day.

   ⃝ correct ⃝ incorrect

10. The star shone.

   ⃝ correct ⃝ incorrect

	EXAMPLE	
	Correct	Incorrect
	⃝	⬤
	ANSWERS	
	Correct	Incorrect
1	⃝	⃝
2	⃝	⃝
3	⃝	⃝
4	⃝	⃝
5	⃝	⃝
6	⃝	⃝
7	⃝	⃝
8	⃝	⃝
9	⃝	⃝
10	⃝	⃝

Integrated Spelling

Name _____

Read each sentence. Mark on the sample answer card the letter of the word that is spelled correctly and makes sense.

Example: Put it over _____.

A their   B ther   C there   D they're

11. I _____ a good joke.

   A herd   B heard   C hurd   D hird

12. Be sure to _____ the door.

   A lok   B louck   C loack   D lock

13. I ate the _____ pie.

   A whole   B hole   C whol   D hoal

14. The _____ took off.

   A plains   B planz   C planes   D playnz

15. I was _____ in Mexico.

   A onse   B once   C wons   D wonce

16. The _____ broke.

   A bored   B bourd   C board   D boared

17. Be honest and _____.

   A fere   B fare   C fear   D fair

18. Always tell the _____.

   A truth   B troth   C thruth   D trooth

19. This _____ is open.

   A areu   B area   C airea   D areah

20. Jack went to _____.

   A cort   B corte   C courte   D court

EXAMPLE

Ⓐ Ⓑ ⬤ Ⓓ

ANSWERS

11 Ⓐ Ⓑ Ⓒ Ⓓ

12 Ⓐ Ⓑ Ⓒ Ⓓ

13 Ⓐ Ⓑ Ⓒ Ⓓ

14 Ⓐ Ⓑ Ⓒ Ⓓ

15 Ⓐ Ⓑ Ⓒ Ⓓ

16 Ⓐ Ⓑ Ⓒ Ⓓ

17 Ⓐ Ⓑ Ⓒ Ⓓ

18 Ⓐ Ⓑ Ⓒ Ⓓ

19 Ⓐ Ⓑ Ⓒ Ⓓ

20 Ⓐ Ⓑ Ⓒ Ⓓ

EMERALD FOREST Unit 2 Review • Harcourt Brace School Publishers

Name _____

TALK TO THE ANIMALS

My Day as a Squirrel

Choose an animal you'd like to be for a day. Then decide where the animal would live. In the jungle? In a pet shop? In a zoo? Think about the animal's daily activities. What other animals might that animal meet? What else might that animal do? After gathering your ideas, write a story about your day as an animal. Draw pictures to go with your story. When you finish, share your story and art with classmates.

TIPS FOR SPELLING SUCCESS If you use possessives in your story, check where you put the apostrophes. Make sure each one is in the right place so that readers don't get confused.

ANIMALS IN DANGER

Help! Many types of animals are in danger of becoming extinct, or dying out. They include the African elephant, the whooping crane, and the California condor. Use recent books and magazine articles to learn about other animals in danger. Find out ways that these animals can be saved. Then help spread the word! Create a large poster that warns people about the dangers some animals face. Persuade your audience to take action to save these creatures.

TIPS FOR SPELLING SUCCESS When writing the names of animals, make sure you capitalize where necessary. Check a dictionary if you're not sure which names require capital letters. Some other words to watch for are listed on the left.

Words
to watch for
....
aware
barely
changing
disappeared
fail
harm
peacefully
protect
situation
stopped

EMERALD FOREST Unit 2 Review • Harcourt Brace School Publishers

LIBRARY ZOO

Create a "library zoo"! On a sheet of construction paper, draw a picture of an animal. Cut out the picture, and write on it the title of an animal book you've enjoyed. Include the author's name, too. Then create a "library zoo" by pasting your animal to a large piece of poster board along with your classmates' animals. Display the poster in the school hallway.

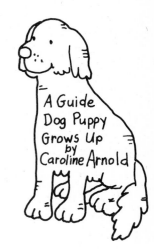

A Guide Dog Puppy Grows Up by Caroline Arnold

TIPS FOR SPELLING SUCCESS If you're not sure how to spell a word in your book title, write the word several ways on scrap paper. Choose the way that looks right. Check a dictionary, if necessary.

ANIMALS IN A ROW

How many kinds of animals can you name? Make a chart like the one below to list different kinds of mammals, fish, birds, reptiles, and insects. But there's a catch! The animal names going across each row must start with the same letter. See how long you can make each list. Use a dictionary to make sure your spelling is correct.

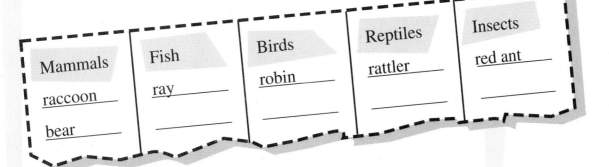

Mammals	Fish	Birds	Reptiles	Insects
raccoon	ray	robin	rattler	red ant
bear				

TIPS FOR SPELLING SUCCESS Check your Spelling Log for the correct spellings of animal names. Add to the log animal names that you might want to use in other writing activities.

Spelling WORDS

1. field
2. either
3. neither
4. friend
5. received
6. eighty
7. believe
8. eighteen
9. weigh
10. chief
11. weight
12. neighbors
13. ceiling
14. thief
15. height
16. weird

YOUR OWN WORDS

Look for other words with *ie* and *ei* to add to the lists. You might find *relief* or *weightless* in a science book. You might use *pierce* or *vein* in a report on leaves.

17. _____
18. _____
19. _____
20. _____

Words Like *field* and *weigh*

Each Spelling Word has *ie* as in *field* or *ei* as in *weigh*. Look at the order of the letters in each word.

Sort the Spelling Words in a way that will help you remember them. One example word is given. Fill in the other one as you are sorting.

belief

The vowels in words like *field* are spelled *ie*.

The vowels in words like *weigh* are spelled *ei*.

EMERALD FOREST "The Plant That Ate Dirty Socks" • Harcourt Brace School Publishers

Integrated Spelling

STRATEGY Workshop

SPELLING CLUES: Mnemonics Try to invent a trick to remember how a word is spelled. For example, to remember that *friend* is spelled with *ie* and not *ei*, this trick might help: I am your fri*end* to the *end*.

Write the Spelling Word that appears in each "trick" sentence below.

1. I saw a <u>thin</u> <u>thief</u>.
2. <u>We</u> b<u>ir</u>ds are <u>weir</u>d.
3. L<u>igh</u>t has no w<u>eigh</u>t.
4. Never bel<u>ie</u>ve a l<u>ie</u>.
5. The friendly <u>chi</u>ef says "<u>hi</u>!"

1. _____
2. _____
3. _____
4. _____
5. _____

6–10. Underline the mnemonic clue for each misspelled word in the journal entry below. Then write each word correctly.

May 4
We sigh when we wiegh our plants. My brother is not happy with ether plant's growth. He doesn't think they are the right hight. If I could find a feild for them, they might grow better. Our new nabors have an empty pasture that I'll explore.

6. _____
7. _____
8. _____
9. _____
10. _____

FUN WITH WORDS Write the Spelling Word that matches each clue.

11. forty plus forty
12. seventeen plus one
13. a package that is accepted by you
14. over your head
15. someone you can always count on
16. not one nor the other

11. _____
12. _____
13. _____
14. _____
15. _____
16. _____

Words to Explore

baffled

logical

disguise

detective

Think about how you might use these words in your writing. You might list *detective* and *disguise* in your Spelling Log under Mystery Words. How might you use them if you were writing a short story?

1. _____

2. _____

3. _____

4. _____

5. _____

_____

_____

_____

_____

_____

_____

_____

6. _____

VOCABULARY WordShop

MYSTERY WORDS You might find these words in a mystery story. Look at the clues on the slips of paper. Write the clue that best fits each column of words below.

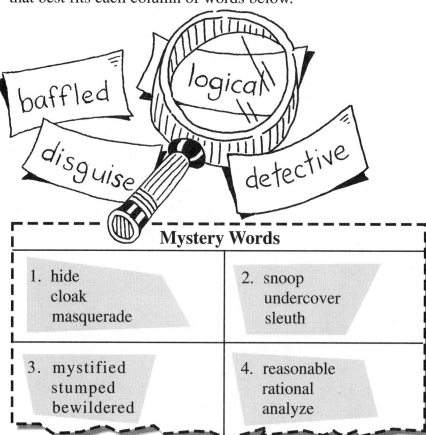

Mystery Words	
1. hide cloak masquerade	2. snoop undercover sleuth
3. mystified stumped bewildered	4. reasonable rational analyze

5. Write at least one more clue for each column.

What's in a Word?

The word *detective* comes from the Latin *de* (un-) *tegare* (cover). Modern detectives try to uncover the truth by searching for clues. *Clue* comes from the Middle English *clewe,* "a spool of thread." What's the connection? In a Greek myth, the hero Theseus goes to the center of a maze to kill a monster called the Minotaur. To help himself find his way back out, Theseus unwinds a spool of thread behind him as he enters the maze. Today, we use clues to help us find our way out of puzzles and problems.

6. Make up a fitting name for a detective. (One example might be *Mr. I. C. Clewes, Private Eye.*)

Name _____

WORD HISTORIES The words under the magnifying glass have interesting histories. Write word that matches each clue below.

nice
café
cloak
neighbor

1. This word, from the Latin *clocca,* "bell," can describe something that is shaped like a bell.
2. This word, which names a place, is the French word for *coffee.*
3. This word comes from the Old English words *nēah* and *gebūr,* meaning "near dweller."
4. This word, from the Latin *nescius,* once meant "ignorant."
5. Think of some good mystery titles using the words under the magnifying glass. Write your titles.

1. _____
2. _____
3. _____
4. _____
5. _____
_____
_____
_____
_____
_____
_____
_____
_____
_____
_____
_____

MYSTERY WORDS Play a mystery word guessing game. Write three one-word clues about a Spelling Word on slips of paper. Show the clues to your partner, one at a time. See if your partner can guess the word.

Words Like *pure* and *worm*

Each Spelling Word has the vowel before *r* sound heard in *pure* or *worm*. Look at the letters that spell those sounds.

Sort the Spelling Words in a way that will help you remember them. One example word is given. Fill in the other one as you are sorting.

Spelling WORDS

1. fur
2. learn
3. worker
4. cure
5. burn
6. earth
7. worm
8. pure
9. return
10. earn
11. world
12. secure
13. burst
14. search
15. worst
16. curve

purely

_____
_____
_____
_____

_____
_____ _____
_____ _____
_____ _____
_____ _____
_____ _____
_____

The vowel before *r* sound in words like *worm* can be spelled *ur*, *ear*, or *or*.

The vowel before *r* sound in words like *pure* is usually spelled *ure*.

YOUR OWN WORDS

Look for other vowel before *r* words to add to the lists. You might find *early* or *curious* in a newspaper headline. You might use *purify* or *curl* in a news report about plants.

17._____
18._____
19._____
20._____

S T R A T E G Y Workshop

PROOFREADING: Using the Dictionary After spelling a word, look at it carefully. If you are not sure if it is spelled correctly, check in the dictionary.

Look at each word below. Decide if it is spelled correctly. If you need help, use the Spelling Dictionary. Then write each word correctly.

1. barst   2. retern   3. puer

4. cerve   5. cure

6–10. Look at the classified ad below. Circle each word that is spelled incorrectly. Then write each word correctly.

Plant Kingdom seeks motivated wurker and offers the opportunity to ern good wages with a sucure employer. On the job, lern how to take care of the most exotic plants in the wold! Call 555-2312 today.

WORKING WITH MEANING Write Spelling Words to replace 11–16.

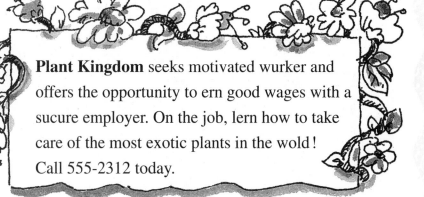

Ugh! This is the 11 plant I ever ate!

It feels as fuzzy as 12 in my mouth.

It's starting to 13 my mouth!

Let's 14 for another plant.

Even a 15 deserves a good meal.

But where on 16 can we find one?

1. _____

2. _____

3. _____

4. _____

5. _____

6. _____

7. _____

8. _____

9. _____

10. _____

11. _____

12. _____

13. _____

14. _____

15. _____

16. _____

Think about how you might use these words in your writing. You might list *finally* and *immediately* in your Spelling Log under Time Words. How might you use them if you were writing a recipe?

VOCABULARY WordShop

SURVIVAL WORDS Use a survival word from the box and the clues below to complete the flowchart.

> thrive   expand   nourishment   preserve

Insects provide ___1___ for carnivorous plants.

The plants ___2___ in marshes.

If we ___3___ the wetlands, their numbers might ___4___ .

1. This word comes from the Latin word *nūtrīre,* "to feed."
2. This word has the long *i* sound.
3. This word has the small word *serve* in it.
4. This word ends with the word *and.*

List other survival words to add to the word web below.

Survival Words

1. _____
2. _____
3. _____
4. _____

5. _____
   _____
6. _____
7. _____
8. _____

Integrated Spelling

What's in a Word?

World and *earth* are synonyms, or words with similar meanings. Both words refer to the planet on which we live. The word *earth* is sometimes spelled with a capital *E* when it refers to the planet. It is spelled *earth* when it refers to soil that plants grow in.

1. Write two other synonyms for the word *earth* or *world*.

1. _____

_____

SYNONYMS On the plant, find the word that is a synonym for each underlined word below. Write each word.

environment

absorb

soil

garden

bloom

2. A plant grows in the <u>ground</u>.

3. Many plants <u>flower</u> in the spring.

4. Growth usually depends on the <u>surroundings</u>.

5. You may see plants in a flower <u>bed</u>.

6. The plants <u>drink</u> the water in the ground in order to grow.

2. _____

3. _____

4. _____

5. _____

6. _____

CHARADES Play charades with two classmates. Act out one of the Spelling Words. Have one classmate keep track of the time while the other tries to guess your word. See how much time goes by until the person guessing writes the correct word on the board. Then swap roles.

Integrated Spelling

1. _found_
2. _join_
3. _clown_
4. _royal_
5. _ground_
6. _coin_
7. _noise_
8. _crowd_
9. _loyal_
10. _around_
11. _choice_
12. _south_
13. _allow_
14. _annoyed_
15. _avoid_
16. _employed_

YOUR OWN WORDS

Look for other words with the vowel sound in *ground* or *coin*. You might find *mouth* or *moist* in a book about rivers. You might use *mountain* or *destroy* in a science report.

17. _____
18. _____
19. _____
20. _____

Name _____

Words Like *ground* and *coin*

Each Spelling Word has the vowel sound heard in *ground* or the vowel sound heard in *coin*. Look at the letters that spell those sounds.

Sort the Spelling Words in a way that will help you remember them. Three example words are given. Fill in the last one as you are sorting.

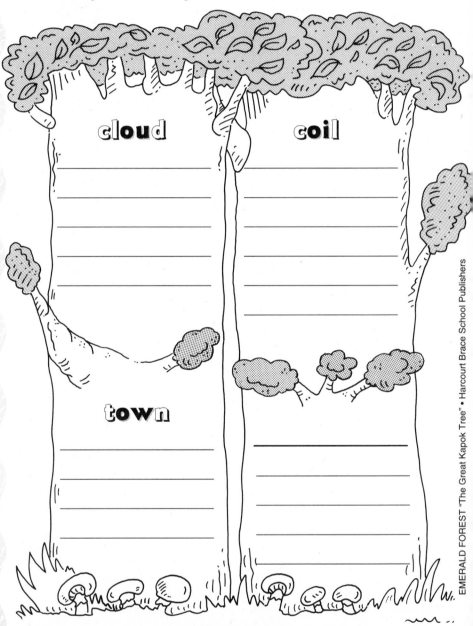

cloud

coil

town

The vowel sound in words like *ground* may be spelled *ou* or *ow*.

The vowel sound in words like *coin* may be spelled *oi* or *oy*.

EMERALD FOREST "The Great Kapok Tree" • Harcourt Brace School Publishers

Integrated Spelling

Name _____

STRATEGY Workshop

PROOFREADING: Checking Vowels Before writing a word, think of the different ways the vowel sound can be spelled. Choose the way that looks correct.

Add the missing vowels. Write the Spelling Words.

1. c _ _ n
2. ann _ _ ed
3. s _ _ th
4. all _ _
5. empl _ _ ed
6. ar _ _ nd

7–10. Proofread the letter. Circle the four words with spelling errors. Then write each word correctly.

> Dear Sam,
>   I hope you will joyn our fight to save the rain forest. We've got to make nose so we'll be heard! The rain forest has been good to us, and we should be loial to it, too. Let's aviod a disaster. Help save the rain forest now!

FUN WITH WORDS Write a Spelling Word to answer each riddle with a rhyme.

11. What do you call a dog that is no longer lost?
    a _____ hound

12. What do you call dirt arranged in a circle? round _____

13. What do you call a noisy group of people?
    a loud _____

14. What do you call earth fit for a king?
    _____ soil

15. What do you call a dress for a circus performer? a _____ gown

16. What does a great singer or speaker have? a _____ voice

1. _____
2. _____
3. _____
4. _____
5. _____
6. _____

7. _____
8. _____
9. _____
10. _____

11. _____
12. _____
13. _____
14. _____
15. _____
16. _____

Words to Explore

emerges
forest
oxygen
pollen

Think about how you might use these words in your writing. You might list *oxygen* and *pollen* in your Spelling Log under Ecology Words. How might you use them if you were writing a plant experiment?

1. _____

2. _____

3. _____

4. _____

5. _____

_____

6. _____

7. _____

8. _____

_____

VOCABULARY WordShop

ECOLOGY WORDS Complete the flowchart. Use the words in the box and the clues below to help you.

| humans | oxygen | animals | forest |

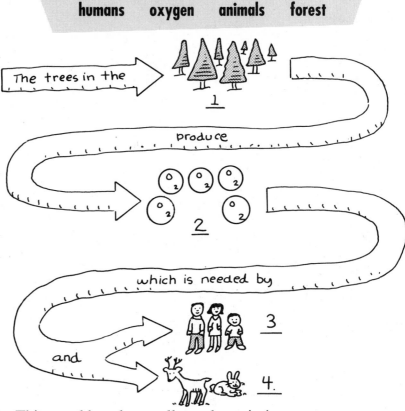

The trees in the ___1___

produce ___2___

which is needed by ___3___

and ___4___

1. This word has the small word *rest* in it.
2. This is one of the few words that has a *y* that stands for a short *i* sound.
3. This word has the small word *man* in it.
4. This word is spelled almost the same way it is in Spanish, *animales*.

Write other ecology words that you would add to each column of the chart below.

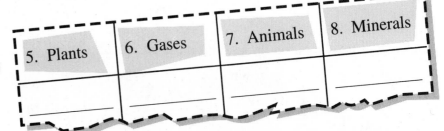

5. Plants	6. Gases	7. Animals	8. Minerals

EMERALD FOREST "The Great Kapok Tree" • Harcourt Brace School Publishers

Integrated Spelling

Name _____

What's in a Word?

A scientific mistake was made when *oxygen* was named. In 1777, the famous French chemist Lavoisier named an element *oxygène.* He chose the Latin words for "forming acid," because he thought that oxygen was necessary for forming all acids. Later, he was proved wrong. Oxygen is an odorless, colorless gas, found in the atmosphere, in water, and in most minerals and living things.

1. If you were the discoverer of oxygen, what would you name it? Give reasons for your choice.

1. _____

_____

2. _____

3. _____

4. _____

5. _____

6. _____

7. _____

ANALOGIES On the tree trunk, find the word that completes each analogy below. Write each word.

2. *Grapes* is to *vine* as _____ is to *tree.*
3. *Fur* is to *animal* as _____ is to *tree.*
4. *Arms* is to *person* as _____ is to *tree.*
5. *Basement* is to *house* as _____ is to *tree.*
6. *Garden* is to *flower* as _____ is to *tree.*
7. *Baby* is to *adult* as _____ is to *tree.*

ANALOGY CHALLENGE Make up some analogies, using the Spelling Words. Write your analogies on a separate sheet of paper. Leave a blank where the Spelling Word fits in the analogy. See if a partner can fill in the blank correctly. Here are some examples:

Palm tree is to *plant* as *dime* is to *coin.*

Satisfied is to *dissatisfied* as *employed* is to *unemployed.*

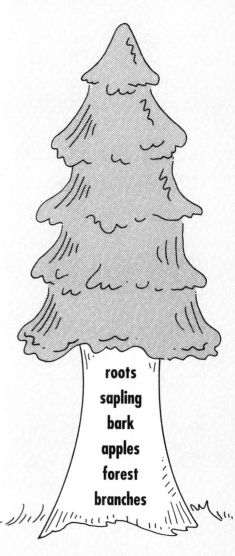

roots

sapling

bark

apples

forest

branches

Integrated Spelling

Spelling WORDS

1. colored
2. moved
3. driving
4. winning
5. stepped
6. chewing
7. tired
8. skating
9. digging
10. spotted
11. swimming
12. happened
13. scared
14. chasing
15. beginning
16. united

YOUR OWN WORDS

Look for other words that end with *-ed* or *-ing* to add to the lists. You might find *weighted* or *living* in a book about diving. You might see *floated* or *bobbing* in a report on the ocean.

17. _____
18. _____
19. _____
20. _____

Words That End with *-ed* and *-ing*

Each Spelling Word ends in *-ed* or *-ing.* Look at how the base word changes when the ending is added.

Sort the Spelling Words in a way that will help you remember them. Four examples are given. Fill in the last two as you are sorting.

played

playing

saved

saving

If a word ends in consonant-*e*, drop the *e* before adding *-ed* or *-ing.*

If a word ends in consonant-vowel-consonant, double the final

consonant before adding *-ed* or *-ing.*

For other words, do not change the base word before

adding *-ed* or *-ing.*

Integrated Spelling

EMERALD FOREST "Down Under, Down Under" • Harcourt Brace School Publishers

STRATEGY Workshop

PROOFREADING: Checking Twice When you proofread, look for and circle words you know are misspelled. Then go back and proofread again. Circle words you might want to check in the dictionary.

1–5. Proofread the list twice. Circle the five words with spelling errors. Write each word correctly.

steped	scared	tired
chewng	running	driveing
floated	skateing	winning
happend	moved	united

6–10. Proofread the brochure twice. Circle the five words with spelling errors. Write each word correctly.

1. _____
2. _____
3. _____
4. _____
5. _____
6. _____
7. _____
8. _____
9. _____
10. _____

Fish Fantasy

Be sure to go swiming and explore the beautiful coral reef. Brilliantly colerd sea urchins and spoted tropical fish use the reef for protection. They won't be chaseing you, so relax and enjoy the view. Remember, no diging is allowed.

WORKING WITH MEANING Write the Spelling Word that means the *opposite* of the underlined word.

11. One family <u>stayed</u>, but another one _____ away.
12. I feel <u>energetic</u>, but my brother is _____.
13. Their team is <u>losing</u>, and our team is _____.
14. Tina is <u>unafraid</u>, but Tony is _____.
15. I am <u>finishing</u> the book, and you are _____ it.
16. The band <u>separated</u> into practice groups which _____ to perform.

11. _____
12. _____
13. _____
14. _____
15. _____
16. _____

Words to Explore

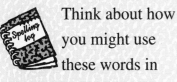

tentacles

barrier

anemone

coral reef

Think about how you might use these words in your writing. You might list *coral reef* and *barrier* in your Spelling Log under Ocean Words. How might you use them if you were writing a script?

1. _____
2. _____
3. _____
4. _____
5. _____
   _____

VOCABULARY WordShop

SEA CREATURE WORDS Can you identify each sea creature or structure in the water? Use the clues and the words in the box for help.

anemone	polyps	coral	shark
1	2	3	4

1. This name comes from the Greek *poly pous,* meaning "many feet."
2. This name comes from the Greek *anemos,* meaning "wind."
3. This name comes from the Hebrew *goral,* meaning "pebble."
4. This name comes from the German *schurke,* meaning "scoundrel."
5. Write a sentence using all the sea creature words.

Now put on your diving gear, and leap into the waves. See how many other sea words you can list.

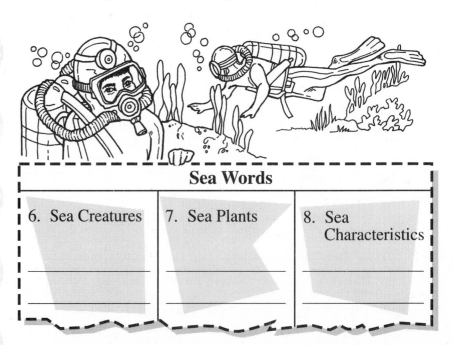

Sea Words

6. Sea Creatures	7. Sea Plants	8. Sea Characteristics
_____	_____	_____
_____	_____	_____

6. _____
   _____
7. _____
   _____
8. _____
   _____

EMERALD FOREST "Down Under, Down Under" • Harcourt Brace School Publishers

Integrated Spelling

What's in a Word?

Spotted comes from the Dutch word *spotte*. The word has many different meanings. One meaning is "located." Another meaning is "marked with spots."

1. Write a sentence about a fish that uses *spotted* in two different ways.

1. _____
_____
_____
_____
_____
_____
_____

MULTIPLE MEANINGS Each word in the fish tank has more than one meaning. Write the word that answers each question. Use a dictionary for help.

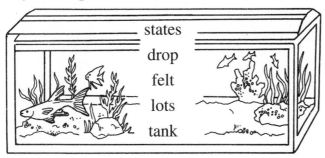

states
drop
felt
lots
tank

2. Which word can mean "a glass container for fish" or "a large combat vehicle"?

3. Which word can mean "a tiny bit of water" or "fall to the ground"?

4. Which word can mean "many" or "areas of land"?

5. Which word can mean "says" or "territories within a federal government"?

6. Which word can mean "touched" or "a soft material"?

2. _____
3. _____
4. _____
5. _____
6. _____

PUZZLER Use six Spelling Words to make a challenging puzzle for your classmates. Write the words across or down. Fill in the empty spaces with other letters. Trade with a classmate, and solve each other's puzzle.

```
s c a r e d l i
a h x e r s t u
b a o l e a t r
c s p m t n e x
d i g g i n g c
d n r o r
e g i a e
a c m c d
```

Changing *y* to *i*

Spelling WORDS

1. copied
2. heavier
3. busiest
4. hurried
5. spied
6. earlier
7. easiest
8. heaviest
9. supplied
10. applied
11. relied
12. prettier
13. funniest
14. prettiest
15. terrified
16. multiplied

YOUR OWN WORDS

Look for other words in which *y* changed to *i* before an ending. You might find *leafier* or *buried* in an almanac. You might see *juicier* or *tastiest* in a recipe.

17. _____
18. _____
19. _____
20. _____

Each Spelling Word has an ending that was added after changing *y* to *i*. Notice how the base word changed when the ending was added.

Sort the Spelling Words in a way that will help you remember them. Two examples are given. Fill in the last one as you are sorting.

tried

sillier

When a word ends in consonant-*y*, change *y* to *i* before adding -*ed*, -*er*, or -*est*.

STRATEGY Workshop

SPELLING CLUES: Spelling Rules Before adding *-ed, -er,* or *-est* to a word that ends in consonant-*y,* remember the rule about changing *y* to *i.* See if the spelling of the word looks right to you.

Add each ending. Write the Spelling Word.

1. rely + ed   2. heavy + er   3. busy + est
4. pretty + er   5. copy + ed

6–10. Read the limerick below. Circle each word that is misspelled. Then write each word correctly.

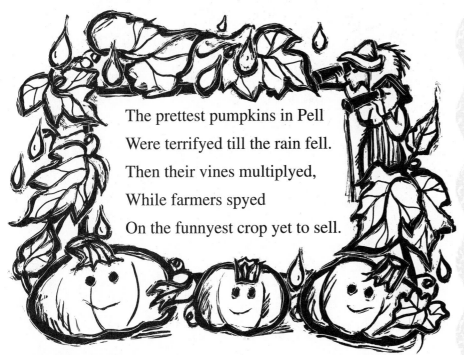

The prettest pumpkins in Pell
Were terrifyed till the rain fell.
Then their vines multiplyed,
While farmers spyed
On the funnyest crop yet to sell.

FUN WITH WORDS Write the Spelling Word that completes each sentence.

11. Last spring I _____ to the store to buy seeds.
12. The store owner _____ me with ten packets.
13. I _____ water to the seeds after I planted them.
14. The seeds sprouted _____ than I thought they would.
15. The _____ watermelon of all grew near the gate.
16. I thought growing vegetables would be hard, but it was the _____ job I ever had!

1. _____
2. _____
3. _____
4. _____
5. _____

6. _____
7. _____
8. _____
9. _____
10. _____

11. _____
12. _____
13. _____
14. _____
15. _____
16. _____

Words to Explore

foreclose

acres

mischief

startling

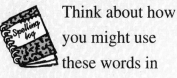

Think about how you might use these words in your writing. You might list *foreclose* and *acres* in your Spelling Log under Property Words. How might you use them if you were writing a sales contract?

1. _____
2. _____
3. _____
4. _____
5. _____
_____
6. _____
_____
7. _____
_____
8. _____
_____
9. _____
_____
10. _____
_____

VOCABULARY WordShop

DESCRIBING WORDS Write the describing word in the box that best answers each question. Use the picture clues below to help you.

| juicy | startling | scrawny | muddy |

1. Which word describes size?
2. Which word describes a liquid quality?
3. Which word describes something that happens?
4. Which word describes appearance?

List at least two describing words you would add to each column of the chart below.

5. Size	6. Texture	7. Happening	8. Color
_____	_____	_____	_____
_____	_____	_____	_____

What's in a Word?

Multiplied comes from the Latin word *multus,* meaning "many." Many words begin with the prefix *multi-*. Each word's meaning is related to the idea of "many."

9–10. Use a dictionary to find two other words that start with *multi-*. Write each word and its meaning.

Name _____

PREFIXES The words on the watermelon have prefixes relating to numbers. Write the word that matches each clue below. Use a dictionary for help.

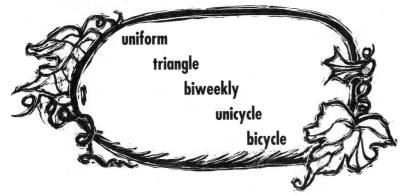

uniform
triangle
biweekly
unicycle
bicycle

1. This word refers to a vehicle with two wheels.
2. This word refers to a vehicle with one wheel.
3. This word refers to a figure with three sides.
4. This word means "happening every two weeks."
5. This word refers to clothing that is all the same.

1. _____
2. _____
3. _____
4. _____
5. _____

DICTIONARY: Base Words The spelling of a word sometimes changes when an ending like -ed, -er, or -est is added. To find the spelling of a word with an ending, you can look up the base word in the dictionary. Write the base word of each word below.

6. sillier
7. worried
8. fanciest
9. occupied
10. whinnied
11. rustiest

6. _____
7. _____
8. _____
9. _____
10. _____
11. _____

-Y RHYMES Work with a classmate. Write a rhyme using the base word of a Spelling Word, for example, *floppy copy*. After you have written six or seven rhymes, make up a silly poem.

Name _____

Practice Test

Read the possible spellings for each word. Mark on the sample answer card the letter of the correct spelling.

Example:

A tabel   B tabul

C tabil   D table

1. A beleive   B beleave
   C believe   D beleeve

2. A weigh   B wiegh
   C weagh   D waigh

3. A esiest   B eziest
   C easyest   D easiest

4. A neither   B niether
   C neether   D neather

5. A serch   B surch
   C search   D sirch

6. A curv   B curve
   C cirve   D cerve

7. A worker   B werker
   C wurker   D wirker

8. A diging   B diggin
   C digging   D digin

9. A sowth   B soth
   C south   D soyth

10. A annoid   B anoyed
    C annode   D annoyed

EXAMPLE

A   B   C   ●

ANSWERS

1   A   B   C   D

2   A   B   C   D

3   A   B   C   D

4   A   B   C   D

5   A   B   C   D

6   A   B   C   D

7   A   B   C   D

8   A   B   C   D

9   A   B   C   D

10   A   B   C   D

EMERALD FOREST Unit 3 Review • Harcourt Brace School Publishers

Name _____

Find the correctly spelled word to complete each phrase. Mark on the sample answer card the letter of the correct word.

Example: _____ quickly

A runing B running C runeng D runnung

11. a squeaky _____

A noyse B noise C noyze D noize

12. a hungry _____

A crowd B croud C croid D crode

13. sandy _____

A urth B irth C earth D erth

14. a _____ of wheat

A feild B feeld C feald D field

15. _____ in a puddle

A steppd B stept C stepped D steped

16. sick and _____

A tired B tierd C tyred D tyered

17. the _____ way

A esiest B eaziest C eziest D easiest

18. _____ to school

A huried B hurried C hurryed D huryed

19. the _____ picture

A prettier B preetier C prettyier D prettyer

20. _____ a map

A copyed B copied C coppied D coppyed

EXAMPLE

Ⓐ ● Ⓒ Ⓓ

ANSWERS

11 Ⓐ Ⓑ Ⓒ Ⓓ

12 Ⓐ Ⓑ Ⓒ Ⓓ

13 Ⓐ Ⓑ Ⓒ Ⓓ

14 Ⓐ Ⓑ Ⓒ Ⓓ

15 Ⓐ Ⓑ Ⓒ Ⓓ

16 Ⓐ Ⓑ Ⓒ Ⓓ

17 Ⓐ Ⓑ Ⓒ Ⓓ

18 Ⓐ Ⓑ Ⓒ Ⓓ

19 Ⓐ Ⓑ Ⓒ Ⓓ

20 Ⓐ Ⓑ Ⓒ Ⓓ

Name _____

LET'S EAT!

Make a class recipe booklet. First, choose your favorite dish. Find out how it's made, either by looking in a cookbook or by getting the recipe from a family member. On a sheet of paper, write out the directions in a how-to paragraph. Your teacher can make copies of your classmates' and your paragraphs. Staple the pages together, and give your recipe booklet a colorful cover. Present it to a family member as a mouth-watering gift!

TIPS FOR SPELLING SUCCESS In your recipe, refer to ingredients clearly. If you write "Add water to it," will readers know what *it* refers to? Make sure to spell your referents correctly.

FLOWERY CARDS

Words
to watch for
· · · · · · · · · · · ·
accept
bright
cheerful
excellent
friendship
happier
lucky
perfect
sincerely
winner

You can create an original "flowery card" in a fun and easy way. Press a flower flat between two pieces of paper in a large book. Then fold a colorful sheet of construction paper in half, and paste the flower to the front. On the inside of your card, write a special message.

TIPS FOR SPELLING SUCCESS When you write your message, check the spelling of words to which you added *-ed, -er, -est,* or *-ing*. Remember the rules you learned for adding those endings. Some other words to watch for are listed on the left.

EMERALD FOREST Unit 3 Review • Harcourt Brace School Publishers

A READING TREE

Make a list of all the good books you've read so far this year. Cut out a large cardboard tree. Then cut out leaves to paste on the tree, using green construction paper. On each leaf, write the name of a book you've read and the name of its author. As you read more books during the year, add more leaves.

TIPS FOR SPELLING SUCCESS When you write the words in your book titles, use memory tricks you have learned for remembering correct spelling. Later, check a dictionary if you're still unsure of the spelling.

END ZONE

How's your spelling? Find out by playing a few rounds of "End Zone." Get together with one or more classmates. One player starts by saying a letter. The next player adds another letter, but tries not to spell a whole word. The third player does the same, and so on. The player who ends up spelling a word loses the round. For example:

Player 2 won the round because the last letter was given by Player 3.

TIPS FOR SPELLING SUCCESS You might want to use a thesaurus to help you. Also, don't forget to use "Study Steps to Learn a Word" to help you learn to spell any words you often misspell.

Compound Words

Each Spelling Word is formed by joining two different words. Look at the two words that make up each compound word.

Sort the Spelling Words in a way that will help you remember them. One example word is given. Fill in the other one as you are sorting.

crash-land

_____
_____
_____

_____

_____   _____
_____   _____
_____   _____
_____   _____
_____   _____
_____   _____

A *compound* is a word made up of two other words.
Some compounds are spelled with the two words
joined together.
Some compounds are spelled with a hyphen between
the two words.

Spelling WORDS

1. anyone
2. good-bye
3. downtown
4. nobody
5. drive-in
6. somebody
7. anyway
8. weekend
9. afternoon
10. however
11. anything
12. backyard
13. sidewalk
14. notebook
15. newspaper
16. basketball

YOUR OWN WORDS

Look for other compound words to add to the lists. You might find *topsoil* or *rainfall* in a science book. You might use *treetop* or *bird's-eye* in a report on birds.

17. _____
18. _____
19. _____
20. _____

Name _____

STRATEGY Workshop

SPELLING CLUES: Word Parts When spelling a compound word, find the two smaller words that it is made of. Spell each word individually, and then put the two words together.

1–4. Combine two words to make a compound word. Write the Spelling Words.

how	bye	no	any
body	good	way	ever

5–9. Read the invitation below. Find each compound word that is spelled incorrectly. Write the word correctly.

> ### The Mayor of Fowler invites you to Safari Days!
> **When:** The adventure begins Saturday afternon and will last the entire week end.
> **Where:** Jungle Park. Follow the sidwalk through the park to the information booth, where sombody will greet you. Admission is free for any one with a local address.

WORKING WITH MEANING Write Spelling Words to replace 10–16.

1. _____
2. _____
3. _____
4. _____

5. _____
6. _____
7. _____
8. _____
9. _____

10. _____
11. _____
12. _____
13. _____
14. _____
15. _____
16. _____

Words to Explore

flood

lava

stampede

volcano

Think about how you might use these words in your writing. You might list *volcano* and *flood* in your Spelling Log under Science Words. How might you use them if you were writing a news report?

1. _____

2. _____

3. _____

4. _____

5. _____

_____

6. _____

_____

7. _____

_____

8. _____

_____

VOCABULARY WordShop

ADVENTURE WORDS Read what the adventure guide has to say. Complete each sentence with an adventure word. Use the words in the box and the clues below for help.

attacks   growling   jungle   stampede

1. This word comes from *jāṅgala* in Sanskrit, meaning "wilderness."

2. This word has the small word *owl* in it.

3. This word has the small word *tack* in it.

4. This word has the small word *stamp* in it.

Now add some other adventure words to the lists.

5. Places	6. Sounds	7. Actions	8. Events
_____	_____	_____	_____

EMERALD FOREST "Jumanji" • Harcourt Brace School Publishers

Integrated Spelling

Name _____

ANIMAL EXPRESSIONS

1. There are many compound words that include animal names. Add to the list at the right. Compare your list with a classmate's list.

What's in a Word?

Have you ever seen an adventure movie at a *drive-in*? Drive-ins, outdoor theaters where people watch movies from their cars, were built in the 1950s. Although there aren't many drive-in theaters left today, there are plenty of drive-in restaurants and banks.

2. Imagine that you have designed a new kind of movie theater. Make up a compound word to name it. Use your word in a sentence about the theater.

2. _____
_____
_____

COMPOUND CARDS Write half of each compound Spelling Word on an index card. Shuffle the cards, and play a card game. Use the rules of Go Fish, dealing out four cards to each player. Try to make matches that form compound words. The player with the most matches wins.

EMERALD FOREST "Jumanji" • Harcourt Brace School Publishers

Spelling W O R D S

1. *untie*
2. *mistake*
3. *unlocked*
4. *disappear*
5. *unseen*
6. *prepaid*
7. *unlucky*
8. *uneven*
9. *misunderstand*
10. *unusual*
11. *discomfort*
12. *uncertain*
13. *prehistoric*
14. *misbehave*
15. *unexpected*
16. *misspelled*

YOUR OWN WORDS

Look for other words with the prefixes *dis-*, *mis-*, *pre-*, and *un-* to add to the lists. You might find *disobey* or *prewar* in your social studies book. You might use *mislead* or *unaware* in an adventure story.

17. _____
18. _____
19. _____
20. _____

Words with Prefixes

Each Spelling Word has the prefix *dis-*, *mis-*, *pre-*, or *un-*. Look at the letters that spell each prefix.

Sort the Spelling Words in a way that will help you remember them. Three example words are given. Fill in the last one as you are sorting.

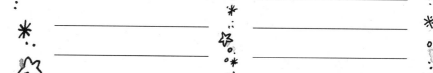

unhappy   **mis**place

_____   _____
_____   _____
_____   _____
_____   _____
_____
_____

disagree
_____   _____
_____   _____

The prefix *un-* means "not" or "the opposite of."

The prefix *mis-* means "wrong" or "bad."

The prefix *dis-* means "the opposite of."

The prefix *pre-* means "before."

STRATEGY Workshop

SPELLING CLUES: Base Words When spelling a word with a prefix, look at the base word that follows the prefix. Make sure it is spelled correctly.

Supply the missing letters. Write each Spelling Word.

1. _ _ even
2. _ _ _ historic
3. _ _ _ take
4. _ _ _ comfort
5. _ _ certain
6. _ _ _ understand

7–10. Un the Alien always writes the opposite of what he means. Read his note. Change each underlined word by adding the prefix *un-*. Write the new words.

Dear Dad,
I had a very <u>usual</u> experience today. My friends and I flew to a(n) <u>seen</u> planet far away. When we <u>locked</u> our spaceship door and stepped out, we found the most <u>expected</u> creatures. They call themselves "humans."

FUN WITH WORDS Write the Spelling Word that describes each picture.

11.

12.

13.

14.

15.

16.

1. _____
2. _____
3. _____
4. _____
5. _____
6. _____

7. _____
8. _____
9. _____
10. _____

11. _____
12. _____
13. _____
14. _____
15. _____
16. _____

Words to Explore

ad lib

device

monotone

UFO

Think about how you might use these words in your writing. You might list *device* in your Spelling Log under Inventions. How might you use it if you were planning a design for a new invention?

1. _____
2. _____
3. _____
4. _____
5. _____
   _____
   _____
6. _____
   _____
   _____
7. _____
   _____
   _____
8. _____
   _____
   _____
   _____

VOCABULARY WordShop

OUTER-SPACE WORDS Complete the story below with the outer-space words in the box. Use the picture clues for help.

| mission | UFO | device | earthlings |

The ___1___ watched a ___2___ in the sky and wondered

what its ___3___ might be. What ___4___ might the aliens be searching for now?

List outer-space words that you would add to the chart below.

5. Places	6. Vehicles	7. Space Events
_____	_____	_____
_____	_____	_____

What's in a Word?

People often make the mistake of writing *misspell* as *mispell*. Here's a trick to help you remember the correct spelling:

Today I met *Miss Pell.*

8. Invent your own memory trick to remember how to spell another Spelling Word. Write your trick.

ANTONYMS For each underlined word below write the word from the spaceship that is an antonym, or opposite.

1. My friends <u>agree</u> that there is life on Mars, but I _____.
2. They've been <u>led</u> to believe in Martians, but I think they've been _____.
3. The existence of life on Earth has been <u>proven</u>, but the existence of life on Mars is still _____.
4. Others are <u>convinced</u> there are Martians, but I am _____.
5. My friends <u>regard</u> their beliefs as fact, but I _____ them completely.

DICTIONARY: Pronunciation A respelling, or special spelling, in the dictionary, tells you how to pronounce a word. Sometimes a vowel is not pronounced the same way it is spelled.

rocket [rok´ it]

Write the correct spelling of each outer-space word. Use a dictionary if you need help.

6. [plan´ it]
7. [shut´ l]
8. [as´ trə · nôt]
9. [mē´ tē · ər]

1. _____
2. _____
3. _____
4. _____
5. _____

6. _____
7. _____
8. _____
9. _____

PREFIX CONCENTRATION Play a Concentration game with a classmate. Write the prefixes and the bases of the Spelling Words on separate index cards and turn the cards face down. Choose two at a time to turn over. The person who makes more matches wins.

EMERALD FOREST "Close Encounter of a Weird Kind" • Harcourt Brace School Publishers

Spelling WORDS

1. funny
2. apply
3. hockey
4. tiny
5. supply
6. alley
7. hurry
8. deny
9. chimney
10. plenty
11. multiply
12. journey
13. country
14. qualify
15. pony
16. beauty

YOUR OWN WORDS

Look for other words that end with -y or -ey to add to the lists. You might use *identify* or *money* in a report about banks. You might find *company* or *occupy* in a social studies book.

17. _____
18. _____
19. _____
20. _____

Words That End with -y and -ey

Each Spelling Word ends with -y or -ey. Look at the letters and listen to how they sound when you say the word.

Sort the Spelling Words in a way that will help you remember them. Two example words are given. Fill in the last one as you are sorting.

key

many

The -ey ending in a word usually has the long e sound.

The -y ending in a word may have the long e or the long i sound.

EMERALD FOREST "The Case of the Million Pesos" • Harcourt Brace School Publishers

Integrated Spelling

STRATEGY Workshop

PROOFREADING: Checking Twice When you proofread, look for and circle words you know are misspelled. Then go back and proofread again. Look for words that you're not sure of.

1–6. Proofread the list twice. Circle the six words with spelling errors. Write the correct spelling for each word.

chimny	funny	beautey	country
suppley	deny	tiny	journy
hockey	qualifey	appley	multiply

7–10. Proofread the poster twice. Circle the four words with spelling errors. Write each word correctly.

NOTICE! Last week a bank robber stole plentey of our money! He got away through the back ally, riding on a poney. If you saw him, hurrey and tell us! **THE BANK**

1. _____
2. _____
3. _____
4. _____
5. _____
6. _____

7. _____
8. _____
9. _____
10. _____

WORKING WITH MEANING Write the Spelling Word that completes each analogy.

11. *Early* is to *late* as *serious* is to _____.
12. *Toy* is to *yo-yo* as *game* is to _____.
13. *Minus* is to *subtract* as *times* is to _____.
14. *Chicago* is to *city* as *United States* is to _____.
15. *Agree* is to *disagree* as *confess* is to _____.
16. *Big* is to *large* as *small* is to _____.

yo-yo

11. _____
12. _____
13. _____
14. _____
15. _____
16. _____

EMERALD FOREST "The Case of the Million Pesos" • Harcourt Brace School Publishers

Words to Explore

alibi

framed

innocent

testify

Think about how you might use these words in your writing. You might list *alibi* and *testify* in your Spelling Log under Law Words. How might you use them if you were writing a court report?

1. _____

2. _____

3. _____

4. _____

5. _____
_____
_____
_____

6. _____
_____
_____

VOCABULARY WordShop

LAW WORDS Write the law word that matches each clue. Use your Spelling Dictionary for help.

framed   innocent   testify   alibi

1. In court, this is what you are until you are proven guilty.

2. This is proof offered by a suspect that he or she was somewhere else at the time of the crime.

3. This phrase means "made to look guilty by others who are lying."

4. This is what witnesses do under oath in court.

5. List other law words that you would add to the word web.

What's in a Word?

The word *testify* means to "bear witness," or tell what you've seen. It comes from two Latin words, *testis*, "witness," and *fiacere*, "to make." The suffix *-fy*, meaning "to make," appears in many other English words, like *amplify*, "to make larger."

6. Think of one other *-fy* word. Write it in a sentence.

EMERALD FOREST "The Case of the Million Pesos" • Harcourt Brace School Publishers

MULTIPLE MEANINGS Each word on the dollar bill has at least two different meanings. For each sentence, write the word that makes sense in both blanks.

1. A dollar _____ landed on the duck's _____ .

2. Can you _____ my _____ for me while I go swimming?

3. I _____ fill the _____ with dirt for the plants.

4. I am proud to _____ that I love my home _____ .

5. The woman _____ from her chair
   to smell the red _____ .

6. The law _____ has a _____
   grasp of the case.

1. _____

2. _____

3. _____

4. _____

5. _____

6. _____

QUICK CHECK Write the Spelling Words on a sheet of paper. Read the words aloud to a partner. Have your partner tell you whether each word ends in *-y* or *-ey*. Then let your partner quiz you in the same way.

Integrated Spelling

Spelling WORDS

1. child's
2. boys'
3. men's
4. sister's
5. brother's
6. parents'
7. teachers'
8. women's
9. father's
10. mother's
11. children's
12. animals'
13. family's
14. teams'
15. people's
16. world's

YOUR OWN WORDS

Look for other words that end in 's or s' to add to the lists. You might find *scientist's* or *cells'* in a science book. You might use *mayor's* or *citizens'* in a social studies report.

17. _____
18. _____
19. _____
20. _____

Possessives

Each Spelling Word is a possessive that ends in *'s* or *s'.* The apostrophe (') indicates ownership. Notice where the apostrophe appears in each word.

Sort the Spelling Words in a way that will help you remember them. Two example words are given. Fill in the last one as you are sorting.

 girl's girls'

_____   _____
_____   _____
_____   _____
_____   _____
_____   _____
_____   _____

_____
_____
_____
_____
_____

Add 's to a singular noun to make it a possessive.

Add an apostrophe (') to a plural noun that ends in -s to make it a possessive.

Add 's to a plural noun not ending in -s to make it a possessive.

EMERALD FOREST "The Gold Coin" • Harcourt Brace School Publishers

Integrated Spelling

STRATEGY Workshop

SPELLING CLUES: Spelling Rules Think about the rules for spelling singular and plural possessives. Follow the rule that applies to each word. Then spell the word.

Make each word into a possessive. Spell the word.

1. mother   2. animals   3. men

4. world   5. teams   6. people

7–10. Read the note below. Change each underlined word to a possessive. Write the word.

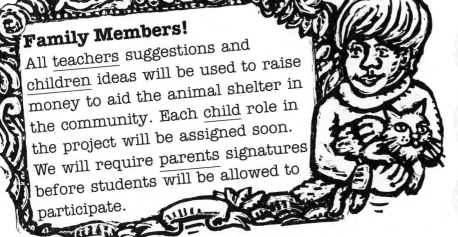

Family Members!
All <u>teachers</u> suggestions and <u>children</u> ideas will be used to raise money to aid the animal shelter in the community. Each <u>child</u> role in the project will be assigned soon. We will require <u>parents</u> signatures before students will be allowed to participate.

WORKING WITH MEANING Write the correct form of the underlined word to make a possessive.

11. After the two <u>boys</u> went to the bank, the _____ new bank accounts were opened.

12. One <u>sister</u> also has an account there, but the other _____ money is not at that bank.

13. Several <u>women</u> work at the bank, and the _____ jobs are very important.

14. My <u>family</u> lives near the bank, but my _____ account is at another bank.

15. Ask my <u>father</u> why this is so, and my _____ answer will explain it.

16. My <u>brother</u> works at another bank, so my _____ money is kept there!

1. _____
2. _____
3. _____
4. _____
5. _____
6. _____

7. _____
8. _____
9. _____
10. _____

11. _____
12. _____
13. _____
14. _____
15. _____
16. _____

Integrated Spelling

Words to Explore

lumbered

ransacked

shriveled

stunned

Think about how you might use these words in your writing. You might list *ransacked* and *stunned* in your Spelling Log under Vivid Verbs. How might you use them if you were writing a short story?

1. _____

2. _____

3. _____

4. _____

5. _____

_____

_____

_____

6. _____

_____

_____

VOCABULARY WordShop

MOVEMENT WORDS Some words tell how people, animals, and things move. Write the movement word in the box that best fits the action in each group of phrases.

crept	huddled	lumbered	twisted

a sleepy elephant
a heavy dinosaur ------ 1
an awkward robot

a thief
a sneaky mouse ------ 2
a growing plant

a swinging rope
an acrobat ----------- 3
someone exercising

a frightened child
someone cold ------- 4
a football team

5. Think of how all the people and things around you move. Add movement words to the word web below.

Movement Words

What's in a Word?

The verb *lumber*, meaning "to walk clumsily or awkwardly," comes from the Middle English word *lome*, or "lame."

6. Write a sentence that uses two meanings of the word *lumber*. Use a dictionary if you need help.

EMERALD FOREST "The Gold Coin" • Harcourt Brace School Publishers

Integrated Spelling

Name _____

SYNONYMS Write the word from the gold coin that answers each question with a rhyme.

nurses'

cats'

president's

teacher's

store's

1. _____
2. _____
3. _____
4. _____
5. _____
6. _____

_____
_____
_____
_____
_____

1. What is the White House? It's the _____ residence.

2. What are pets owned by the head of the class?
   They are the _____ creatures.

3. What are wallets used by hospital workers?
   They are _____ purses.

4. What do people step on in a shop?
   They walk on the _____ floors.

5. What were the kittens wearing on their heads?
   They wore the _____ hats.

6. Now, make up a question and rhyme of your own.

SPELLING RHYMES Make up some rhymes like the ones above, using Spelling Words. Write a question for each rhyme. See if a classmate can answer the question. Be sure the apostrophe is in the correct place in each answer.

Integrated Spelling

Name _____

Practice Test

Read the possible spellings for each word.
Mark on the sample answer card the letter of
the correct spelling.

Example: A pencul   B pensil
               C pensul   D pencil

1. A downtoun   B dountown
   C dountoun   D downtown

2. A drivein   B drive in
   C drive-in   D drivin

3. A jurney   B journi
   C journy   D journey

4. A weekend   B week-end
   C week end   D weakend

5. A good by   B goodbi
   C good-bye   D goodbie

6. A mispelled   B misspelled
   C misspeled   D mispeled

7. A disapear   B disappere
   C disappear   D dissapear

8. A untye   B unty
   C untiey   D untie

9. A prepayed   B prepade
   C prepaid   D prepayde

10. A childs'   B child's
    C childs   D childe's

EXAMPLE
Ⓐ Ⓑ Ⓒ ●

ANSWERS
1 Ⓐ Ⓑ Ⓒ Ⓓ
2 Ⓐ Ⓑ Ⓒ Ⓓ
3 Ⓐ Ⓑ Ⓒ Ⓓ
4 Ⓐ Ⓑ Ⓒ Ⓓ
5 Ⓐ Ⓑ Ⓒ Ⓓ
6 Ⓐ Ⓑ Ⓒ Ⓓ
7 Ⓐ Ⓑ Ⓒ Ⓓ
8 Ⓐ Ⓑ Ⓒ Ⓓ
9 Ⓐ Ⓑ Ⓒ Ⓓ
10 Ⓐ Ⓑ Ⓒ Ⓓ

Integrated Spelling

Name _____

Mark on the sample answer card the letter of the underlined word in each sentence that is spelled wrong.

Example:

Sam <u>rode</u> his <u>bycycle</u>.
     a.   b.

11. Let's <u>hury</u> through the <u>alley</u>.
       a.   b.

12. Does <u>any one</u> have a <u>basketball</u>?
         a.   b.

13. There is a <u>tiny</u> <u>supplie</u> of food.
         a.   b.

14. Did you <u>qualify</u> for the <u>hocky</u> team?
        a.   b.

15. The <u>pone</u> is acting <u>funny</u> today.
       a.   b.

16. My <u>misstake</u> caused <u>discomfort</u> for me.
      a.   b.

17. The <u>mens'</u> hats are in the <u>boys'</u> room.
      a.   b.

18. My <u>fathers'</u> office is in our <u>family's</u> home.
     a.   b.

19. The <u>womens'</u> cars are at my <u>sister's</u> house.
      a.   b.

20. Are <u>animals'</u> dreams like <u>peoples'</u> dreams?
      a.   b.

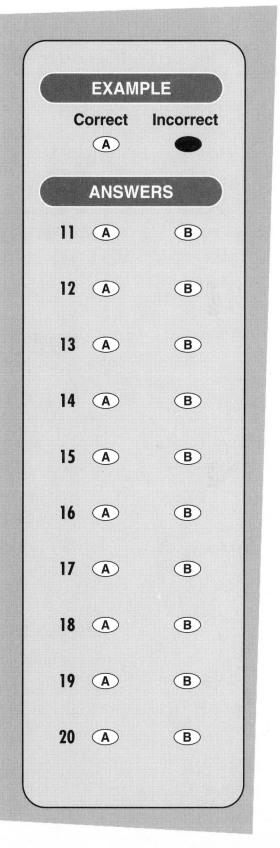

EXAMPLE

Correct   Incorrect
  Ⓐ   ●

ANSWERS

11 Ⓐ   Ⓑ

12 Ⓐ   Ⓑ

13 Ⓐ   Ⓑ

14 Ⓐ   Ⓑ

15 Ⓐ   Ⓑ

16 Ⓐ   Ⓑ

17 Ⓐ   Ⓑ

18 Ⓐ   Ⓑ

19 Ⓐ   Ⓑ

20 Ⓐ   Ⓑ

Name _____

A GREAT DISCOVERY!!

Words to watch for

amazement
bones
curious
happened
history
museum
piece
protect
realize
scientist

Imagine that you recently made an unusual discovery. What was it? That's up to you to decide. It might be a new kind of plant or a very old buried treasure. Write an essay that tells what your discovery looks, sounds, smells, feels, or tastes like. Tell how you happened to find it and what you plan to do with it. The whole world is waiting to learn about your discovery!

TIPS FOR SPELLING SUCCESS In your essay, be sure your subjects and verbs agree. Check the spelling of each subject and verb for agreement. Some other words to watch for are listed on the left.

DETECTIVE'S ORDERS

So you want to be a detective, eh? That's fine. But you'll need special equipment that detectives use. What would you like? Perhaps a giant magnifying glass. Maybe a pen that writes in invisible ink. Are you looking for a two-way radio wristwatch? Whatever your needs, you can order them from The Detective Store. Write a business letter to the store, listing the equipment you need. Be sure to describe each item clearly.

TIPS FOR SPELLING SUCCESS Look for compound words, such as *wristwatch,* that you may have used in your letter. Check to see that each word within the compound is spelled correctly. Of course, check the spelling of all other words as well.

EMERALD FOREST Unit 4 Review • Harcourt Brace School Publishers

FLIPPING OVER BOOKS!

Here's a simple way for your class to "flip over" new books. On a sheet of paper, write the title of a favorite book you've read this year. Below the title, write the author's name. Then write one or two sentences that tell what the book is about. Take a second sheet of paper, and place it over the first. Tape along the top so that the front sheet can be flipped up. Work with classmates to organize your papers on a bulletin board. In your free time, go to the bulletin board and "flip over" books your classmates have enjoyed!

TIPS FOR SPELLING SUCCESS When you write your book descriptions, use vivid verbs to capture the interest of other readers. Check the spelling of the verbs and other words you use.

Encyclopedia Brown Gets His Man
by Donald Sobol
A clever boy cracks many cases by sniffing out small details.

FILL IN THE MIDDLE

Here's a game that will "compound" your fun! Think of two compound words. The last part of one word must be the first part of the other word; for example, *newspaper* and *paperback*.

Choose a partner and give him or her this puzzle:

news _____ *back*

See if your partner can guess the word that goes in the middle. Then let your partner make up a compound puzzle for you to solve!

TIPS FOR SPELLING SUCCESS Refer to your Spelling Log for lists of compound words. Remember to add to the log compound words that you misspell frequently.

Spelling WORDS

1. bodies
2. parties
3. calves
4. plays
5. pennies
6. leaves
7. copies
8. keys
9. wolves
10. cherries
11. chemicals
12. knives
13. berries
14. shelves
15. decades
16. memories

YOUR OWN WORDS

Look for other plural words to add to the lists. You might find *valleys* and *skies* in a weather report. You might use *strays* or *hooves* in a report about farm life.

17. _____
18. _____
19. _____
20. _____

Plurals

Each Spelling Word is a plural form. A word is **plural** when it names more than one thing. Look at the ending of each word to see how the plural form is spelled.

Sort the Spelling Words in a way that will help you remember them. Three example words are given. Fill in the last one as you are sorting.

halves
_____
_____
_____
_____
_____

spies
_____
_____
_____

days
_____
_____
_____
_____

To form most plurals, just add *s*.

To form plurals of words ending in:

. . . *f* or *fe*, change *f* to *v* and add *es*.

. . . consonant-*y*, change *y* to *i* and add *es*.

EMERALD FOREST "A River Ran Wild" • Harcourt Brace School Publishers

Integrated Spelling

STRATEGY Workshop

SPELLING CLUES: Spelling Rules Think about the rules for spelling plurals.
Follow the rule that applies to each word spelled in plural form.

Make each word into a plural. Write the word.

1. copy   2. shelf   3. chemical
4. memory   5. play   6. calf

7–11. The author of the sign below forgot to use plurals.
Find the five words that should be plural. Write them
correctly.

1. _____
2. _____
3. _____
4. _____
5. _____
6. _____

7. _____
8. _____
9. _____
10. _____
11. _____

Attention! Have all your party by the river! Have fun picking wild berry and cherry. Perfect for all special holidays! Room for any number of body. All ages. Costs just penny per person. Call now!

FUN WITH WORDS Write a SpellingWord that fits each item
below.

12. A century has ten of them. _____
13. Folktales often feature them. _____
14. Cars and pianos need them. _____
15. Tables and trees often have them. _____
16. Chefs need a sharp set of them. _____

12. _____
13. _____
14. _____
15. _____
16. _____

VOCABULARY WordShop

TIME WORDS Use the words in the box and the diagram to complete the sentences below.

Words to Explore

descendant
century
generation
year

Think about how you might use these words in your writing. You might list *descendant* and *generation* in your Spelling Log under Social Studies Words. How might you use them if you were writing about your family history?

1. _____

2. _____

3. _____

4. _____

5. _____
_____
_____

6. _____
_____
_____

7. _____
_____
_____

decade   century   generation   year

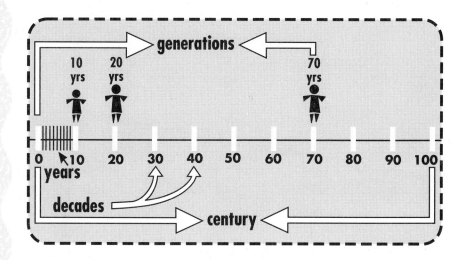

1. The Latin root *cent,* meaning "one hundred" is a part of _____.

2. One _____ is equal to 365 days.

3. The Greek word part *deca* meaning "ten" is a part of _____.

4. A _____ separates parents and their children.

Now think of some other Time Words. Add them to the lists.

5. Calendar Words	6. Clock Words	7. Historical Time Periods
_____	_____	_____
_____	_____	_____
_____	_____	_____

EMERALD FOREST "A River Ran Wild" • Harcourt Brace School Publishers

Integrated Spelling

What's in a Word?

For generations wolves have been popular characters in folktales and legends. The word *wolf* comes from the Old English word *wulf* and has similar spellings in other languages.

1–2. Think of famous literary wolves. Try to write at least two book titles or names of famous wolves you know from literature.

1. _____

_____

_____

2. _____

_____

_____

ANIMAL WORD HISTORIES Many names of animals have interesting word histories. If necessary, use a reference source to help you answer these questions.

Which animal's name comes from

3. the Old English *bera,* which means "brown animal"?

4. the Old English *deor,* which means "wild animal"?

5. the Old English *duncan,* which means "to dive"?

6. the Greek *skiaoura,* which means "shadow tail"?

7. the Algonquian *arakun,* which means "scratcher"?

8. the Spanish *el lagarto,* which means "the lizard"?

9. Work with a group to research animal names with interesting word histories: penguin, lobster, walrus, rhinoceros, porcupine, armadillo, quetzal, otter, and porpoise. You may want to make a book of animal histories with your group.

3. _____

4. _____

5. _____

6. _____

7. _____

8. _____

9. _____

_____

_____

_____

_____

_____

_____

_____

EMERALD FOREST "A River Ran Wild" • Harcourt Brace School Publishers

Spelling WORDS

1. paper
2. motor
3. collar
4. letter
5. butter
6. doctor
7. corner
8. cellar
9. wonder
10. manner
11. labor
12. matter
13. calendar
14. answer
15. harbor
16. remember

YOUR OWN WORDS

In what book might you read about an *otter* becoming a *neighbor*? In the same book, look for other words that end with the schwa-*r* sound.

17. _____
18. _____
19. _____
20. _____

Words That End Like *answer* and *motor*

Each Spelling Word ends with the schwa-*r* (/ər/) sound heard at the end of *answer* and *motor.* Look at the letters that spell the schwa-*r* sound.

Sort the Spelling Words in a way that will help you remember them. Two example words are given. Fill in the last one as you are sorting.

actor

dollar

The schwa-*r* sound in words like *answer* and *motor* may be spelled *er, or,* or *ar.*

Integrated Spelling

STRATEGY Workshop

PROOFREADING: Using a Dictionary When you proofread, use a dictionary for words you are unsure of. Make corrections that are needed.

1–5. Proofread the list. Circle the five words that are misspelled. Then write the correct spelling for each word.

harber	matter	collar	calender
remember	celler	paper	cornar
manner	parlor	sugar	wondor

6–10. Proofread the note card below. Circle the five words that are misspelled. Check and write their correct spellings.

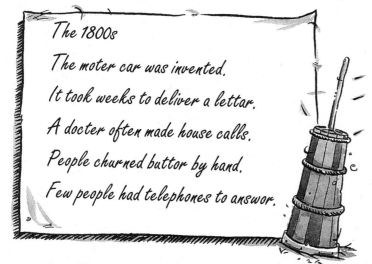

The 1800s

The moter car was invented.

It took weeks to deliver a lettar.

A docter often made house calls.

People churned buttor by hand.

Few people had telephones to answor.

FUN WITH WORDS Write the Spelling Word that answers each riddle with a rhyme.

11. What do you do after you recall November?
    _____ December

12. What do you call a shirt part that costs a hundred pennies? a dollar _____

13. What do you call bonnets and crowns? hatter _____

14. What do you call a book of etiquette? a _____ planner

15. What do you call someone whose hobby is origami?
    a _____ shaper

16. What do you call working with the person next door?
    neighbor _____

1. _____
2. _____
3. _____
4. _____
5. _____

6. _____
7. _____
8. _____
9. _____
10. _____

11. _____
12. _____
13. _____
14. _____
15. _____
16. _____

Words to Explore

attentive

contradicting

driven

yoked

Think about how you might use these words in your writing. You might list *driven* and *yoked* in your Spelling Log under Action Verbs. How might you use them if you were writing a history report?

1. _____
2. _____
3. _____
4. _____

5. _____
_____
_____
_____
_____

6. _____
_____
_____
_____
_____
_____

VOCABULARY WordShop

PRAIRIE WORDS What were the duties of settlers on the prairie? Write the prairie word that completes each sentence. Use a dictionary for help.

wagon

sunbonnet

yoked

dugout

1. The father built a _____ to live in.
2. The son _____ the cattle to plow land.
3. The mother rode to the store in a _____.
4. The daughter sewed a _____ to wear on sunny days.

5. List more pioneer duties for the prairie word web below.

Pioneer Duties

What's in a Word?

A *bonnet* was a hat worn outdoors by women, girls, and babies. It was usually made of soft material and tied under the chin. A *sunbonnet* of the type Laura Ingalls Wilder or other settler women might have worn had a brim in front and a ruffle in back to keep the hot sun off both the face and the neck.

6. List other compound words that might have been used by pioneers on the prairie.

EMERALD FOREST "On the Banks of Plum Creek" • Harcourt Brace School Publishers

COMPOUND CONFUSION Match the boxes on the left and the right to make words settlers might have used on the prairie.

1. hay ☐   ☐ pint
2. sun ☐   ☐ out
3. run ☐   ☐ stacks
4. half ☐   ☐ bonnet
5. dug ☐   ☐ away

6–10. Write five more compound words using the following parts.

sun   half

NAME HISTORIES The words on the wagon come from people's names. Write the word that answers each question.

diesel
sideburns
sandwich
saxophone
cardigan

11. The Earl of Sandwich put meat between two slices of bread. What do we call his invention?

12. Adolphe Sax invented a musical instrument made of brass. What is it called?

13. Rudolf Diesel invented a kind of engine that uses oil as fuel. What is its name?

14. General Ambrose Burnside grew long, bushy hair on the sides of his face. What do we call this hair today?

15. The Earl of Cardigan wore a knitted sweater that buttoned in the front. What is it called?

1. _____
2. _____
3. _____
4. _____
5. _____

6. _____
7. _____
8. _____
9. _____
10. _____

11. _____
12. _____
13. _____
14. _____
15. _____

SPELLING TRICKS Read the Spelling Words to a partner as he or she writes them. Then switch roles. For any word either of you spells incorrectly, make up a memory trick to help you remember the spelling. (For example, "A coll*ar* goes *ar*ound your neck.")

Integrated Spelling

Spelling WORDS

1. button
2. often
3. trouble
4. animal
5. listen
6. natural
7. lemon
8. bottle
9. golden
10. example
11. ribbon
12. several
13. possible
14. eleven
15. national
16. special

YOUR OWN WORDS

Look for other words ending in /əl/ or /ən/ to add to the lists. You might find *vegetable* or *onion* in a book about food. You might use *metal* or *union* in a report on industry.

17. _____
18. _____
19. _____
20. _____

Words That End Like *bottle* and *eleven*

Each Spelling Word ends with the schwa-*l* (/əl/) sound heard at the end of *bottle* and *animal* or the schwa-*n* (/ən/) sound heard at the end of *eleven* and *button*. Look at the letters that spell these sounds.

Sort the Spelling Words in a way that will help you remember them. Three example words are given. Fill in the last one as you are sorting.

cott**on**

final
_____
_____
_____
_____
_____

rott**en**
_____
_____
_____
_____
_____

_____
_____
_____
_____
_____

The schwa-*l* sound in words like *animal* and *bottle* may be spelled *al* or *le*.

The schwa-*n* sound in words like *eleven* and *often* may be spelled *on* or *en*.

Integrated Spelling

STRATEGY Workshop

SPELLING CLUES: Comparing Spellings When you're unsure how to spell a word, try writing it a few ways. Choose the way that looks right to you.

Look at the possible spellings. Write the spelling that looks correct.

1. natureal natural
2. often ofton
3. national nationle
4. possable possible
5. ribben ribbon
6. example exampal

7–10. Complete the poster. Write the correct spellings.

Important meeting tomorrow at ___7___ (elevn/eleven) o'clock! We will discuss ___8___ (several/severl) ways to cut down on pollution. Without action, we're in ___9___ (trobel/trouble)! Come speak out, and ___10___ (listen/liston) to others, too.

1. _____
2. _____
3. _____
4. _____
5. _____
6. _____
7. _____
8. _____
9. _____
10. _____

WORKING WITH MEANING Write the Spelling Word that completes each analogy.

11. *Jacket* is to *zipper* as *shirt* is to _____.
12. *Carrot* is to *vegetable* as *dog* is to _____.
13. *Red* is to *tomato* as *yellow* is to _____.
14. *Tin* is to *can* as *glass* is to _____.
15. *Silver* is to *silvery* as *gold* is to _____.
16. *Common* is to *ordinary* as *unusual* is to _____.

11. _____
12. _____
13. _____
14. _____
15. _____
16. _____

Words to Explore

billowing

furnaces

smokestacks

torches

Think about how you might use these words in your writing. You might list *furnaces* and *smokestacks* in your Spelling Log under Factory Words. How might you use them if you were writing a factory description?

1. _____

2. _____

3. _____

4. _____

5. _____
_____
_____

6. _____
_____
_____

7. _____
_____
_____
_____

VOCABULARY WordShop

FACTORY WORDS Complete the sentences. Use the flowchart and a dictionary to help you.

smokestacks   torches   molten   furnaces

1 ____   2 ____   3 ____   4 ____

1. Hand-held _____ are used to start a fire.
2. The _____ send heat to the steel vat.
3. The _____ steel glows red and flows like lava.
4. Smoke travels up through the tall _____.

For the flowchart below, write two more steps that might be part of the production process in a shirt factory.

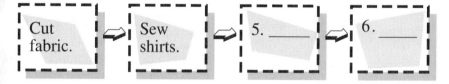

| Cut fabric. | ⇨ | Sew shirts. | ⇨ | 5. _____ | ⇨ | 6. _____ |

What's in a Word?

A *lemon* is a small, sour fruit with a juicy pulp. But in slang, or informal language, *lemon* has another meaning. It refers to something poorly made that doesn't work well.

7. Write why you think *lemon* has come to mean "a poor product."

EMERALD FOREST "No Star Nights" • Harcourt Brace School Publishers

SLANG Each of the words on the loaf of bread has a slang meaning as well as a formal meaning. Write the word that matches the clues below.

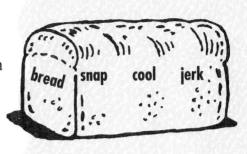

1. In formal language, this word means "to pull suddenly." In slang, it means "a stupid person."
2. In formal language, this word means "a baked food made of flour." In slang, it means "money."
3. In formal language, this word means "chilly." In slang, it means "very appealing."
4. In formal language, this word means "to break quickly." In slang, it means "an easy job."

1. _____

2. _____

3. _____

4. _____

DICTIONARY: Multiple Meanings A dictionary gives slang meanings as well as formal meanings. Write the slang meaning for each word below.

dough [dō] *n.* **1** a soft, thick mixture of flour and liquid **2** *slang* __5__	**sack** [sak] **1** *n.* a bag **2** *v. slang* __6__
loaded [lō´ did] *adj.* **1** bearing a load **2** *slang* __7__	**sock** [sok] **1** *n.* a short stocking **2** *v. slang* __8__

rich
to fire from a job
to hit
money

QUICK CHECK Write these word beginnings down the left side of a sheet of paper:

ribb–	anim–	gold–	possib–
lem–	list–	examp–	elev–
oft–	natur–	butt–	nation–
troub–	bott–	sever–	speci–

On the right side of the page, write these endings:

–on	–en	–le	–al

5. _____

6. _____

7. _____

8. _____

Without looking at your spelling list, draw a line between each word beginning and the correct ending. Check your answers.

Spelling WORDS

1. everybody
2. everything
3. nearby
4. ice cream
5. nowhere
6. somehow
7. everyone
8. firefighter
9. airport
10. fireplace
11. motorcycle
12. home run
13. windshield
14. themselves
15. totem pole
16. nevertheless

YOUR OWN WORDS

Look for other compound words to add to the lists. You might find *rain forest* or *heat wave* in a science book. You might use *deerskin* or *handmade* in a report on Native American crafts.

17. _____
18. _____
19. _____
20. _____

More Compound Words

Each Spelling Word is formed by joining two or more different words. Look at the words that make up each compound.

Sort the Spelling Words in a way that will help you remember them. One example word is given. Fill in the other one as you are sorting.

doghouse

A compound is a word made up of two or more other words.

Some compounds are spelled with the two words joined together.

Some compounds have a space between the two words.

Integrated Spelling

EMERALD FOREST "Totem Pole" • Harcourt Brace School Publishers

STRATEGY Workshop

SPELLING CLUES: Word Parts When spelling a compound word, find the smaller words that it is made up of. Spell each word individually and then put the words together.

1–5. Combine two or three words to make a compound word. Write the Spelling Words.

no	near	home	never	selves	where
run	the	them	less	by	

1. _____
2. _____
3. _____
4. _____
5. _____

6–10. On the note below, circle each compound word that is spelled incorrectly. Write the entire word correctly.

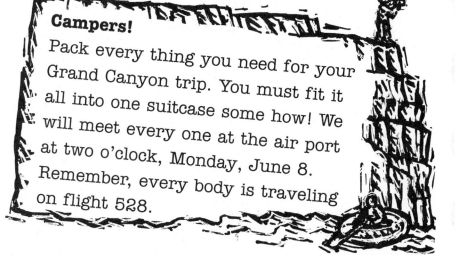

Campers!
Pack every thing you need for your Grand Canyon trip. You must fit it all into one suitcase some how! We will meet every one at the air port at two o'clock, Monday, June 8. Remember, every body is traveling on flight 528.

6. _____
7. _____
8. _____
9. _____
10. _____

WORKING WITH MEANING Write the Spelling Word that names each picture.

11.
12.
13.

14.
15.
16.

11. _____
12. _____
13. _____
14. _____
15. _____
16. _____

Words to Explore

ceremony

clan

reservation

traditions

Think about how you might use these words in your writing. You might list *clan* and *traditions* in your Spelling Log under Social Studies Words. How might you use them if you were writing a family history?

1. _____

2. _____

3. _____

4. _____

5. _____
_____

6. _____
_____

VOCABULARY WordShop

NATIVE AMERICAN WORDS Look at the Native American words in the word web. Write the word that completes each sentence in the letter. Use a dictionary for help.

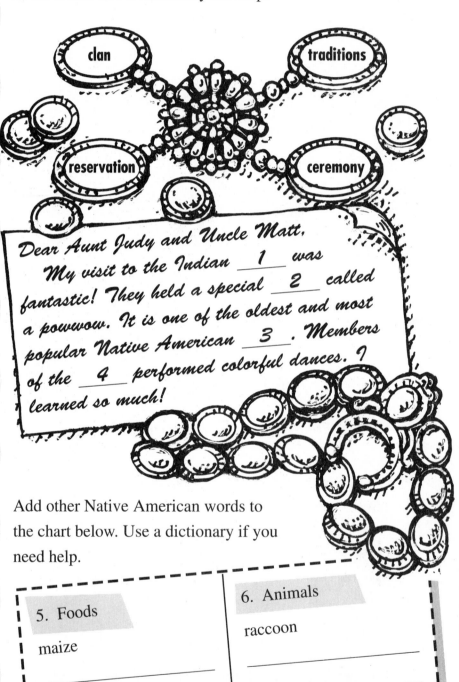

Dear Aunt Judy and Uncle Matt,
  My visit to the Indian __1__ was fantastic! They held a special __2__ called a powwow. It is one of the oldest and most popular Native American __3__. Members of the __4__ performed colorful dances. I learned so much!

Add other Native American words to the chart below. Use a dictionary if you need help.

5. Foods	6. Animals
maize	raccoon
_____	_____
_____	_____

EMERALD FOREST "Totem Pole" • Harcourt Brace School Publishers

Integrated Spelling

What's in a Word?

Fireplace combines two words from two different cultures: *fȳr* (Old English for "fire") and *plateia* (Greek for "plaza" or "wide place").

1. There are many compound words that include *fire*. List as many as you can.

NAME THAT STATE! Many of our state names came from Native American words. Name the states whose names were formed from the words below.

Word	Meaning	State
kentake	"meadowland"	2. _____
quonectacut	"river of pines"	3. _____
minni sota	"sky-tinted water"	4. _____
ouiscousin	"meeting of the rivers"	5. _____
ayuxwa	"beautiful land"	6. _____
al-ay-es-ka	"great country"	7. _____

WORD CHAINS Make a word chain with a classmate. Start by writing one Spelling Word. Invite your classmate to use a letter in that word to write another Spelling Word, across or down. Now take your turn, and write a third word. Keep going as long as you can. How many Spelling Words can you link in one chain?

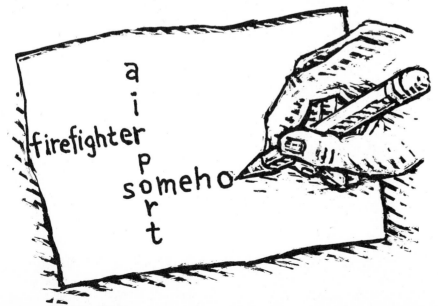

1. _____
_____
_____
_____
_____
_____
_____
_____
_____
_____
_____

2. _____

3. _____

4. _____

5. _____

6. _____

7. _____

Name _____

Practice Test

Read the four groups of words. Find the underlined word that is spelled wrong. Mark on the sample answer card the letter for that word.

Example:

A a big <u>magazine</u> B two <u>swings</u>
C a great <u>vacashon</u> D <u>writing</u> a book

1. A red <u>berrys</u> B tired <u>bodies</u>
   C <u>calves</u> grazing D a bowl of <u>cherries</u>

2. A cracked <u>windshield</u> B <u>nearby</u> store
   C brick <u>fire place</u> D loud <u>motorcycle</u>

3. A sharp <u>knifes</u> B golden <u>leaves</u>
   C happy <u>memories</u> D stock the <u>shelves</u>

4. A birthday <u>parties</u> B ten <u>pennys</u>
   C <u>plays</u> the violin D hungry <u>wolves</u>

5. A <u>answer</u> the phone B bread and <u>butter</u>
   C new <u>calender</u> D go to the <u>cellar</u>

6. A shirt <u>collar</u> B stop at the <u>corner</u>
   C call a <u>doctor</u> D ships in the <u>harber</u>

7. A hard <u>labor</u> B mail a <u>lettur</u>
   C a small <u>matter</u> D tissue <u>paper</u>

8. A brave <u>firefighter</u> B everyone <u>came</u>
   C tall <u>totempole</u> D first <u>home run</u>

9. A <u>animal</u> habits B a broken <u>bottel</u>
   C sew the <u>button</u> D <u>eleven</u> players

10. A set an <u>example</u> B a <u>golden</u> sunset
    C <u>lemen</u> pie D <u>listen</u> carefully

EXAMPLE

Ⓐ Ⓑ ⬤ Ⓓ

ANSWERS

1 Ⓐ Ⓑ Ⓒ Ⓓ

2 Ⓐ Ⓑ Ⓒ Ⓓ

3 Ⓐ Ⓑ Ⓒ Ⓓ

4 Ⓐ Ⓑ Ⓒ Ⓓ

5 Ⓐ Ⓑ Ⓒ Ⓓ

6 Ⓐ Ⓑ Ⓒ Ⓓ

7 Ⓐ Ⓑ Ⓒ Ⓓ

8 Ⓐ Ⓑ Ⓒ Ⓓ

9 Ⓐ Ⓑ Ⓒ Ⓓ

10 Ⓐ Ⓑ Ⓒ Ⓓ

EMERALD FOREST Unit 5 Review • Harcourt Brace School Publishers

Name _____

If you're planning a vacation soon, here are a few tips to <u>remembar</u> so you
                                                                              11

avoid <u>troubil</u>. First, try to plan <u>everthing</u> in advance. Make spare <u>copys</u> of your
      12   13   14

house and car <u>keyz</u> in case you lose a set. Make reservations at a <u>moter</u> lodge
               15   16

or motel before you leave home. That's because motels are <u>oftun</u> booked and
                                                                  17

hard to get into at the last minute. If you're leaving from the <u>air port</u>, give yourself
                                                                18

plenty of time to catch your flight. Sometimes <u>sevaral</u> hours are not too many. Finally,
                                                19

bring snack food along. But beware of something like <u>icecream</u>, which will melt
                                                      20

quickly if not eaten right away!

Each underlined word above is spelled wrong. Mark the letter next to the correct
spelling below.

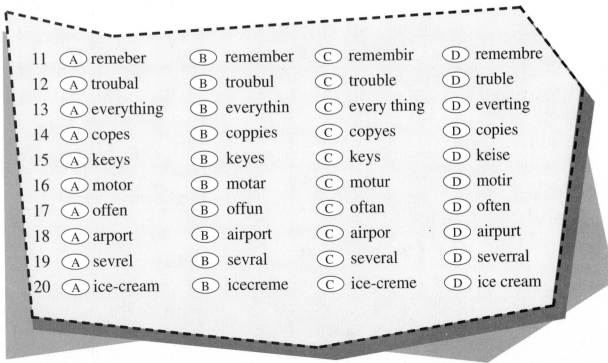

11	Ⓐ remeber	Ⓑ remember	Ⓒ remembir	Ⓓ remembre
12	Ⓐ troubal	Ⓑ troubul	Ⓒ trouble	Ⓓ truble
13	Ⓐ everything	Ⓑ everythin	Ⓒ every thing	Ⓓ everting
14	Ⓐ copes	Ⓑ coppies	Ⓒ copyes	Ⓓ copies
15	Ⓐ keeys	Ⓑ keyes	Ⓒ keys	Ⓓ keise
16	Ⓐ motor	Ⓑ motar	Ⓒ motur	Ⓓ motir
17	Ⓐ offen	Ⓑ offun	Ⓒ oftan	Ⓓ often
18	Ⓐ arport	Ⓑ airport	Ⓒ airpor	Ⓓ airpurt
19	Ⓐ sevrel	Ⓑ sevral	Ⓒ several	Ⓓ severral
20	Ⓐ ice-cream	Ⓑ icecreme	Ⓒ ice-creme	Ⓓ ice cream

Name _____

PLACE TO PLACE

Are you a traveler? Perhaps you've been to another town, state, or country. Or maybe you've visited two places in your own town, like the park and the zoo. Choose two places you have been. Draw a picture of each place. Then write a paragraph that tells how the places are alike or different. Later, you may wish to read your paragraph aloud and share your pictures with classmates.

TIPS FOR SPELLING SUCCESS Check to see if you've written any plural words in your paragraph. Remember the rules you learned for spelling plurals. Make sure the spellings are correct.

LET'S GO PLACES!

Imagine you are the head of a travel agency. Make a poster that will convince customers to travel to your favorite vacation spot. Draw pictures or cut out magazine pictures of the place of your choice. Paste the pictures on a large piece of poster board. Then write one or more paragraphs that give customers strong reasons for going there. Put your writing on the poster.

Words
to watch for
....
adventure
beautiful
completely
dining
especially
favorite
highway
magical
nicest
outstanding

TIPS FOR SPELLING SUCCESS Try to use as many colorful words as possible when trying to persuade your customers. Be sure to place all adverbs where they belong. Then check for spelling. Some words to watch for are listed on the left.

Name _____

WHERE'S THE STORY

Where do the books you've read take place? Keep track with a "book map." Use a large map of the world, or draw your own world map. On individual index cards, write the title of each book you've read this year. Also write the name of the author and the place where the story occurs. Pin the card on the map in its proper spot. Add to your book map throughout the year!

TIPS FOR SPELLING SUCCESS The names of some cities, states, and countries can be tricky to spell. If you're unsure of a spelling, try a few different ways. Then check the geographical section of the dictionary.

WHAT STARTS WITH...?

You can have lots of fun playing CATEGORY. Make a chart like the one below. See if you can fill in each box with a name starting with the letter indicated. One box has already been filled in.

	C	A	T	E	G	O	R	Y
town or city					Golden Acres			
state								
country								

TIPS FOR SPELLING SUCCESS You might want to use a thesaurus to help you. Also, don't forget to use Study Steps to Learn a Word to help you learn to spell words you often misspell.

Spelling WORDS

1. careless
2. colorful
3. payment
4. sadness
5. helpless
6. helpful
7. hopeless
8. cheerful
9. movement
10. happiness
11. useless
12. beautiful
13. agreement
14. wilderness
15. endless
16. wonderful

YOUR OWN WORDS

Look for other words with the suffixes -less, -ful,-ment, and -ness to add to the lists. You might find *lifeless* or *careful* in a science book. You might use *environment* or *dryness* in a weather report.

17. _____
18. _____
19. _____
20. _____

Words with Suffixes

Each Spelling Word has the suffix -*less, -ful, -ment,* or -*ness.* Look at the letters that spell each suffix.

Sort the Spelling Words in a way that will help you remember them. Three example words are given. Fill in the last one as you are sorting.

homeless

joyful

government

The suffix -*less* means "without."

The suffix -*ful* means "full of."

The suffix -*ment* means "the act of or state of being."

The suffix -*ness* means "the state of being."

Integrated Spelling

STRATEGY Workshop

SPELLING CLUES: Comparing Spellings When spelling a word with a suffix, look at the base word and at the suffix. Make sure both are spelled correctly.

Look at the base word and the suffix in each word. Write the correct spelling.

1. agreement   agreemint
2. wilderness   wildernes
3. colorfull   colorful
4. helppless   helpless
5. paymint   payment
6. endless   enless

1. _____
2. _____
3. _____
4. _____
5. _____
6. _____

7–10. Look at the base word and the suffix in each underlined word. Write the correct spelling.

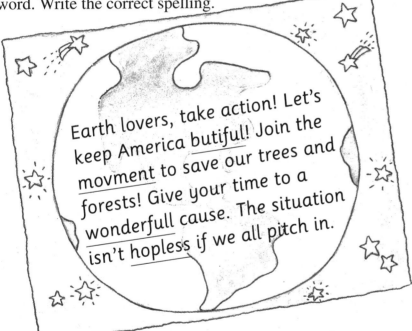

Earth lovers, take action! Let's keep America butiful! Join the movment to save our trees and forests! Give your time to a wonderfull cause. The situation isn't hopless if we all pitch in.

7. _____
8. _____
9. _____
10. _____

WORKING WITH MEANING Write the Spelling Word that can replace the underlined words in each sentence.

11. If we are without care, our forests will disappear.
12. It would be full of help if fewer trees were cut.
13. It's without use to try to change things unless everyone pitches in.
14. Let's bring a state of being happy into our lives.
15. A pretty country will make people full of cheer.
16. Keep our landscape green, and avoid a state of being sad!

11. _____
12. _____
13. _____
14. _____
15. _____
16. _____

Words to Explore

haze
hydrant
peered
shrieking

Think about how you might use these words in your writing. You might list *haze* in your Spelling Log under Weather Words. How might you use them if you were writing a report about a fire?

1. _____
2. _____
3. _____
4. _____

5. _____
_____
_____
6. _____
_____
_____

VOCABULARY WordShop

ATMOSPHERE WORDS Use the clues and words in the box to help you identify the different conditions or products of the atmosphere.

| haze | smog | snowflakes | foggy |

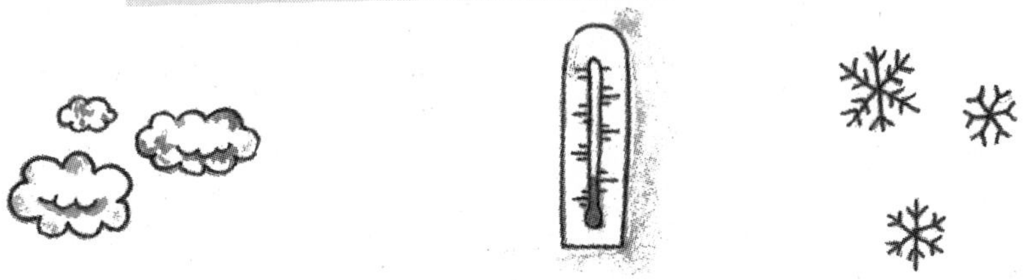

clouds   +   freezing temperatures   =   1

clouds near Earth   =   2

smoke   +   fog   =   3

dust   +   air   =   4

Add other atmosphere words to the chart.

5. Natural Conditions
_____
_____

6. Results of Pollution
_____
_____

Integrated Spelling

What's in a Word?

Helpful and *helpless* both have the base word *help*. The word *help* has several synonyms, including *assist* and *aid*.

1. Write a sentence that tells about a rescue in the forest. Use the word *help, assist,* or *aid.*

THE VIVID SYNONYMS CHALLENGE Write a complete word in as many boxes in the chart as you can. Each word you write must begin with the letter at the top and be a synonym of the word on the left. Good luck!

	s	g	c
2. said			
3. move			
4. look			
5. ate			

SUFFIX CONCENTRATION Play a Concentration game with a classmate, the same way you played with prefixes earlier. Write the suffix and base for each Spelling Word on a separate index card. Turn the cards face down. The one who makes more matches wins.

Integrated Spelling

1. _____
_____
_____
_____
_____
_____

2. _____
_____
_____
_____
_____

3. _____
_____
_____

4. _____
_____
_____
_____

5. _____
_____
_____
_____
_____

Spelling Words

1. *better*
2. *market*
3. *summer*
4. *silver*
5. *ladder*
6. *picnic*
7. *rabbit*
8. *master*
9. *sudden*
10. *public*
11. *wallet*
12. *seldom*
13. *copper*
14. *member*
15. *puppet*
16. *lumber*

YOUR OWN WORDS

Look for other VCCV words to add to the lists. You might find *rotten* or *garbage* in an article about trash. You might use *current* or *harbor* in a report on oceans.

17. _____
18. _____
19. _____
20. _____

Spelling Patterns: VCCV Words

Each Spelling Word has a VCCV letter pattern in the middle of the word. Find this letter pattern in each word.

Sort the Spelling Words in a way that will help you remember them. One example word is given. Fill in the other one as you are sorting.

hotter

Some words have a VCCV letter pattern.
The two consonants in the middle of the word
may be the same, or they may be different.

Integrated Spelling

EMERALD FOREST "A River Dream" • Harcourt Brace School Publishers

Name _____

S·T·R·A·T·E·G·Y Workshop

PROOFREADING: Working Together When you proofread, work with a partner. Read the words aloud as your partner looks at the spelling. Then trade jobs.

Write the spelling that looks correct to you. Check to see whether your partner agrees.

1. markit/market
2. seldom/seldem
3. summer/sumer
4. suden/sudden
5. picknick/picnic
6. puppet/pupet

1. _____
2. _____
3. _____
4. _____
5. _____
6. _____

7–10. Find the four incorrectly spelled words in the letter. Circle and spell them correctly. See whether your partner agrees.

Dear Aunt Molly,
   Thanks for the siver fishing rod! I am now a membar of the fishing club. When I first tried out the rod at the puplic lake, I caught a wallit!

7. _____
8. _____
9. _____
10. _____

FUN WITH WORDS Write the Spelling Word that answers each question with a rhyme.

11. What do you call an improved note in the mail?
    a _____ letter
12. What do you call a quicker boss? a faster _____
13. What do you call a metal popcorn maker? a _____ popper
14. What do you call a numeral made from a piece of wood?
    a _____ number
15. What do you call a bunny's activity? a _____ habit
16. What do you call an angrier climbing device?
    a madder _____

11. _____
12. _____
13. _____
14. _____
15. _____
16. _____

Words to Explore

reel

gills

cast

trout

Think about how you might use these words in your writing. You might list *cast* and *reel* in your Spelling Log under Sports Words. How might you use them if you were writing directions for fly fishing?

1. _____

2. _____

3. _____

4. _____

5. _____
_____

6. _____
_____

7. _____
_____

8. _____
_____
_____

VOCABULARY WordShop

FISHING WORDS Complete each sentence with a word from the list on the left. Use the picture clues and your Spelling Dictionary to help you.

1. The fishers _____ their lines into the water.
2. They wind the line on a _____ at the base of the rod.
3. A _____ swims nearby.
4. The creature breathes through its _____.

Add more outdoor words to the chart below.

5. Fishing
6. Hiking
7. Camping

8. If you wanted to find more words about fishing, hiking, and camping, where could you look?

EMERALD FOREST "A River Dream" • Harcourt Brace School Publishers

Name _____

What's in a Word?

Picnic comes from the French words *pique-nique,* meaning "to pick a thing of little importance." Did you know *picnic* is also the name of a kind of meat?

1. Write a sentence about a real or an imaginary picnic you once attended. Use the word *picnic.*

1. _____
   _____
   _____
   _____
   _____
   _____

MULTIPLE MEANINGS Each word on the fish has more than one meaning. Write the word that could go in both blanks in each sentence.

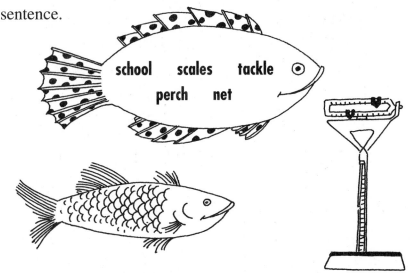

school   scales   tackle
perch   net

2. A fisher uses equipment called _____; a football player tries to _____ the opponent.

3. A fisher scoops fish with a _____; a businessperson tries to _____ a great profit.

4. Some fish have _____; doctors measure their patients' weight on _____.

5. Fish swim together in a _____; children go to _____ to learn.

6. One kind of fish is called _____; birds _____ on a branch when they are resting.

2. _____
3. _____
4. _____
5. _____
6. _____

VOCABULARY CHALLENGE Write each Spelling Word in a sentence. That's the easy part. Here's the challenge: Each sentence must include the word *trout* and must make sense. Work with a partner. Put some of your sentences together. Make up a crazy story about a trout.

Spelling Patterns: More VCCV Words

Each Spelling Word has a VCCV letter pattern in the middle of the word. Find the letter pattern in each word.

Sort the Spelling Words in a way that will help you remember them. One example word is given. Fill in the other one as you are sorting.

EMERALD FOREST "Mufaro's Beautiful Daughters" • Harcourt Brace School Publishers

number
_____ _____
_____ _____
_____ _____
_____
_____ _____
_____ _____
_____ _____
_____

Some words have a VCCV letter pattern.

The two consonants in the middle of the word may be

the same, or they may be different.

Spelling WORDS

1. hidden
2. signal
3. traffic
4. robber
5. subject
6. grammar
7. lesson
8. temper
9. tunnel
10. plastic
11. channel
12. blanket
13. contest
14. cannon
15. forward
16. squirrel

YOUR OWN WORDS

Where might you read about a *garden* or a *poppy*? In that same resource, look for other VCCV words to add to the lists. You might use *hobby* or *pastime* in a report on your interests.

17. _____
18. _____
19. _____
20. _____

STRATEGY Workshop

PROOFREADING: Checking Spelling After spelling a word, look at the way you've written it. Decide whether it looks right to you. Try another spelling if you think it looks wrong.

Decide whether each word is spelled correctly. Write each word the right way.

1. tempur
2. plastick
3. grammer
4. chanel
5. lesson
6. tunel

7–10. Find the four misspelled words in the sign below. Write each word correctly.

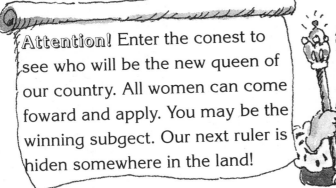

Attention! Enter the conest to see who will be the new queen of our country. All women can come foward and apply. You may be the winning subgect. Our next ruler is hiden somewhere in the land!

FUN WITH WORDS Write the Spelling Word that names each picture.

11.
12.
13.
14.
15.
16.

1. _____
2. _____
3. _____
4. _____
5. _____
6. _____
7. _____
8. _____
9. _____
10. _____

11. _____
12. _____
13. _____
14. _____
15. _____
16. _____

Words to Explore

advise

bountiful

considerate

praise

Think about how you might use these words in your writing. You might list *advise* and *praise* in your Spelling Log under Vivid Verbs. How might you use them if you were writing a letter to a friend?

1. _____
2. _____
3. _____
4. _____

5. _____
_____
_____
_____
_____

6. _____
_____
_____
_____
_____

VOCABULARY WordShop

CHARACTER TRAITS Write the character trait from the box that best describes each person below.

> worthy   bountiful   clever   considerate

1. This person can play two games of chess at the same time and win both of them!
2. This person delivered newspapers for many years and won a special award from the newspaper.
3. This person visits her elderly neighbors every day to see how they are doing.
4. This person gives a lot of money to different charities every year.

5. Write the name of a character that you would like to write a folktale about. Then list traits that the character would have.

Character

What's in a Word?

Contest can be pronounced two ways. Stress the first syllable, and you're talking about a race or a competition between two or more opponents. Stress the second syllable, and you're talking about fighting against something.

6. Write a sentence that uses both meanings of *contest*.

Integrated Spelling

Name _____

PRONUNCIATION AND MEANING Each word on the crown can be pronounced two different ways and has two different meanings. Write the word that matches each clue below.

1. When its first syllable is stressed, it means "a music album." When its second syllable is stressed, it means "to write down or to put on tape."
2. When its first syllable is stressed, it means "a license." When its second syllable is stressed, it means "to allow."
3. When its first syllable is stressed, it means "a machine for harvesting grain." When its second syllable is stressed, it means "to join."
4. When its first syllable is stressed, it means "behavior." When its second syllable is stressed, it means "to lead an orchestra."

conduct   permit
record   combine

1. _____

2. _____

3. _____

4. _____

DICTIONARY: Pronunciation The dictionary tells which syllable to stress for each word meaning. Read the entries below. Write the correct word, including a mark to show which syllable is stressed.

> **content** [kən·tent´] *adj.* satisfied
> **content** [kon´ tent] *n.* what something contains
> **forearm** [fôr´ ärm] *n.* the arm from wrist to elbow
> **forearm** [fôr·ärm´] *v.* to prepare in advance
> **object** [ob´ jekt] *n.* a thing that can be seen or touched
> **object** [əb·jekt´] *v.* to oppose or disagree

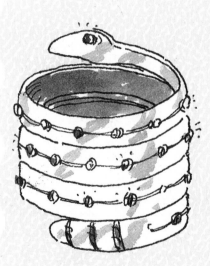

5. Sasha wore a snake bracelet on her _____.
6. "I want to own that pretty _____," said her sister.
7. "I don't _____ to giving it to you," Sasha said.
8. "If you are happy, I feel _____."

5. _____

6. _____

7. _____

8. _____

QUICK CHECK Read the Spelling Words aloud as a partner writes them. Put a check mark beside any word your partner spells incorrectly. Then switch roles. Practice writing any words that have check marks beside them.

Spelling Patterns: VCV Words

Each Spelling Word has a VCV letter pattern in the middle of the word. Find the letter pattern in each word. Listen to the sounds it spells.

Sort the Spelling Words in a way that will help you remember them. Two example words are given. Fill in the last one as you are sorting.

become

_____
_____
_____
_____
_____

timer

_____
_____
_____
_____
_____

_____
_____
_____
_____

Some words have a VCV pattern in the middle of the word.

The vowel in the first syllable of the word may

produce the long *e*, long *i*, or long *o* sound.

Spelling Words

1. equal
2. tiger
3. polar
4. legal
5. silent
6. motion
7. fever
8. pilot
9. notice
10. detail
11. minor
12. solar
13. minus
14. female
15. focus
16. cedar

YOUR OWN WORDS

Look for other words with the VCV pattern to add to the lists. You might find *motor* or *mileage* in a book about cars. You might find *zero* or *bisect* in a math book.

17. _____
18. _____
19. _____
20. _____

Integrated Spelling

STRATEGY Workshop

SPELLING CLUES: Sounding It Out When you spell a word, sound out the individual syllables. Use the letters that spell the sounds you hear.

Supply the missing vowels. Write the words.

1. l _ g _ l
2. n _ t _ c e
3. s _ l _ r
4. f _ v _ r
5. p _ l _ r

6–10. Find the five misspelled words in the letter, and sound them out. Then write the words correctly.

1. _____
2. _____
3. _____
4. _____
5. _____

Dear Coach Miller,

You said the last detale for starting our baseball team was choosing a name. I say we name our team after the tigar. There's a minur league team with the same name. We could wear striped uniforms that fans would focas on. Can we vote on this moshen at our next meeting?

6. _____
7. _____
8. _____
9. _____
10. _____

WORKING WITH MEANING Write the Spelling Word that completes each analogy.

11. *Train* is to *engineer* as *airplane* is to _____.
12. *Same* is to *different* as *odd* is to _____.
13. *Big* is to *little* as *noisy* is to _____.
14. *Addition* is to *plus* as *subtraction* is to _____.
15. *Metal* is to *iron* as *wood* is to _____.
16. *Stop* is to *halt* as *detect* is to _____.

11. _____
12. _____
13. _____
14. _____
15. _____
16. _____

Words to Explore

fouls

innings

shortstop

strike

Think about how you might use these words in your writing. You might list *shortstop* and *strike* in your Spelling Log under Baseball Words. How might use them if you were writing a sports report?

1. _____

2. _____

3. _____

4. _____

5. _____

_____

6. _____

_____

7. _____

_____

8. _____

_____

VOCABULARY WordShop

BASEBALL WORDS Complete the sentences with words from the box. Use a dictionary for help.

| bunt | plate | pitch | shortstop |

1. At the ball game, the batter stands at the _____.
2. The pitcher throws the first _____.
3. The batter decides to _____ instead of swinging fully.
4. A _____ rushes in to catch the baseball.

Glebswatch is from the planet Gloobswutch. He's studied English carefully, but he's never seen a baseball game before. Answer his questions about baseball words with multiple meanings. Use a dictionary for help.

5. *Out?* Out? Why must that player leave the field?

6. The ball is *foul?* That's disgusting!

7. The announcer said it is a *fly.* Do you use insects in this game?

8. *Strike?* Did he hit someone?

EMERALD FOREST "Shortstop from Tokyo" • Harcourt Brace School Publishers

Integrated Spelling

What's in a Word?

Minor has several meanings. It means "a person under the legal age of adulthood." It also means "not very important," as in a *minor accident.* In baseball, a team may be in the *minor leagues.*

1. Write a sentence using the word *minor* in two ways.

1. _____
_____
_____
_____
_____
_____

MULTIPLE MEANINGS Each word on the bat has more than one meaning. Write the word that fits each clue. Use a dictionary for help.

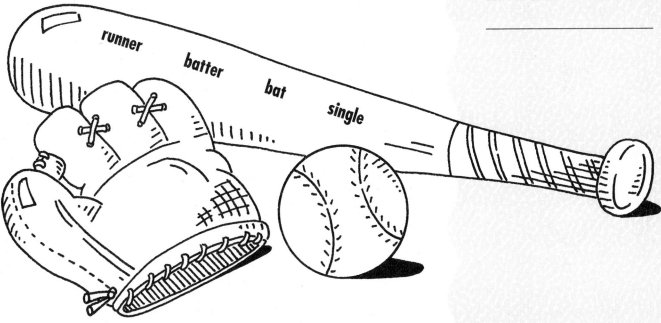

2. This is a stick for hitting a baseball.
   It's also a flying mammal.

3. This is a baseball player trying to hit the ball.
   It's also a mixture of ingredients used when baking a cake.

4. This is a hit that advances a player one base.
   It also describes an unmarried person.

5. This is a player who's advancing from base to base.
   It's also the blade on an ice skate.

2. _____

3. _____

4. _____

5. _____

ALPHA CO-OP Have a race with a partner: see who can write the Spelling Words in alphabetical order more quickly. Then work together to be sure the words are in the proper order.

Integrated Spelling

Spelling Patterns: More VCV Words

Each Spelling Word has a VCV letter pattern in the middle
Find the letter pattern in each word. Listen to the sounds.

Sort the Spelling Words in a way that will help you remember
them. Three example words have been given. Fill in the last
one as you are sorting.

1. baker
2. music
3. duties
4. basic
5. major
6. pirate
7. sofa
8. bacon
9. humor
10. nation
11. silence
12. nature
13. future
14. patient
15. pupil
16. native

YOUR OWN WORDS

Look for other words with
the VCV pattern to add to
the lists. You might find
bison or *tiger* in a book
about animals. You might
use *super* or *design* when
describing a piece of art.

17. _____
18. _____
19. _____
20. _____

safer

_____   _____
_____   _____
_____   _____
_____   _____
_____   _____

rider   **token**

_____   _____
_____   _____
_____   _____
_____   _____
_____   _____
_____
_____

Some words have a VCV pattern in the middle.

The vowel in the first syllable of the word may be pronounced

as long *a*, long *i*, long *o*, or long *u*.

EMERALD FOREST "On the Pampas" • Harcourt Brace School Publishers

Name _____

STRATEGY Workshop

PROOFREADING: Using the Dictionary When you proofread, circle any words that do not look correct. Use a dictionary to check their spellings.

1–5. Which words do not look right to you? Circle five. Check and write the correct spellings.

dutys   music   nashion

baker   pupil   baseec

humor   mager   soffa

6–9. Circle the four words that are misspelled in the journal entry. Check their spellings and write the words correctly.

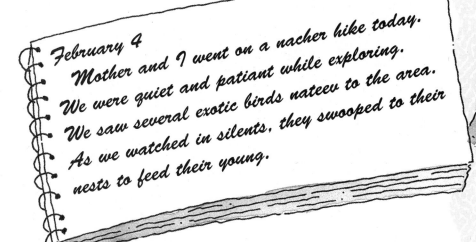

February 4
Mother and I went on a nacher hike today. We were quiet and patiant while exploring. We saw several exotic birds nateev to the area. As we watched in silents, they swooped to their nests to feed their young.

WORKING WITH MEANING Write Spelling Words to complete the conversation below.

What job would you like at some 10 time?

A pig farmer "brings home the 12"!

As a 14 teacher you'd play the high C's.

With your sense of 16, you should be a comedian!

I hear all "really takes the cake".

As a 13, I'd travel the high seas.

Maybe I'll just remain a 15 in school.

1. _____
2. _____
3. _____
4. _____
5. _____

6. _____
7. _____
8. _____
9. _____

10. _____
11. _____
12. _____
13. _____
14. _____
15. _____
16. _____

Words to Explore

gauchos

lasso

pampas

siesta

Think about how you might use these words in your writing. You might list *gauchos* and *siesta* in your Spelling Log under Spanish Words. How might you use them if you were writing a social studies report?

1. _____

2. _____

3. _____

4. _____

5. _____

_____

_____

6. _____

_____

_____

7. _____

_____

VOCABULARY WordShop

SPANISH WORDS Write the word from the list on the left that matches each clue. Use the picture clues and your Spelling Dictionary for help.

1. This brief afternoon nap refreshes people in Spain and Mexico.
2. These treeless plains are found in Argentina.
3. These Indian and Spanish cowboys live on the South American plains.
4. This long rope with a noose at one end is used to catch cattle or horses.

Many of our words from other cultures name foods, restaurants, or cooking styles. See how many words you can add to the chart.

What's for Dinner?

5. Spanish taco	6. French éclair	7. Japanese tofu

Integrated Spelling

What's in a Word?

The words *native, nation,* and *nature* share the same origin. They all come from the Latin *nascī,* meaning "to be born."

1. List four other words that come from the same base word.

1. _____
_____
_____
_____

WORD HISTORIES Many words in English have been "borrowed" from Spanish and other languages. Write the word from the outline of South America that matches each clue below. Use your dictionary for help.

2. This Spanish word refers to a golden horse with a white mane and tail.

3. This Spanish word refers to a woolen blanket worn over one shoulder.

4. This French word refers to a soft, flat, round cap made of wool.

serape
éclair
sauerkraut
beret
palomino
kindergarten

2. _____

3. _____

4. _____

5. _____

6. _____

7. _____

5. This French word refers to a small, long pastry filled with custard or whipped cream.

6. This German word refers to a class of young children around four to six years old.

7. This German word refers to chopped cabbage that has a sharp taste.

TEAM ANALOGIES Work with a partner. Write analogies that can be completed with Spelling Words. Challenge another team to complete your analogies.

Example: *Salt* is to *pepper* as *bacon* is to *eggs.*

EMERALD FOREST "On the Pampas" • Harcourt Brace School Publishers

Name _____

Practice Test

Read the possible spellings for each word.
Mark on the sample answer card the letter of
the correct spelling.

Example:

A telaphone   B telephone
C teliphone   D telifone

1. A beutiful   B beautyful
    C beautiful   D butiful

2. A happyness   B happiness
    C hapiness   D happines

3. A movment   B movemant
    C movement   D moviment

4. A music   B muzic
    C musqic   D moosic

5. A markit   B markat
    C marcket   D market

6. A publick   B publik
    C public   D pubblic

7. A wallet   B wallit
    C walet   D walit

8. A grammer   B gramer
    C grammur   D grammar

9. A notise   B notece
    C notice   D notase

10. A subgect   B subject
    C subjict   D subjact

EXAMPLE

A ● C D

ANSWERS

1 A B C D

2 A B C D

3 A B C D

4 A B C D

5 A B C D

6 A B C D

7 A B C D

8 A B C D

9 A B C D

10 A B C D

EMERALD FOREST Unit 6 Review • Harcourt Brace School Publishers

Name _____

Read each sentence. Mark on the sample answer card the correctly spelled word to complete the sentence.

Example: The eagle _____.

  A sored   B sord   C soared D sared

11. The _____ cook dropped a knife.

  A careles   B carless   C careless D carelest

12. Be _____.

  A silent   B silunt   C silant   D sielent

13. The _____ ate an acorn.

  A squrrel   B squirrel C squirel   D squiral

14. See the _____.

  A tiger   B tyger   C tieger   D tigar

15. Make no _____.

  A moshen B motion   C moshin   D motian

16. A _____ noise scared me.

  A suddan   B suddin   C sudden   D suden

17. A _____ is ready.

  A pupil   B pupal   C pupile   D popil

18. She's a _____.

  A bakier   B bacer   C baker   D bayker

19. Be _____.

  A patiant   B patien   C pashunt D patient

20. I won the _____.

  A conest   B contest   C contess   D contst

EXAMPLE			
A	B	●	D

ANSWERS			
11	A	B	C	D
12	A	B	C	D
13	A	B	C	D
14	A	B	C	D
15	A	B	C	D
16	A	B	C	D
17	A	B	C	D
18	A	B	C	D
19	A	B	C	D
20	A	B	C	D

Name _____

PLAYDREAMING!

Have you ever heard of "playdreaming"? It means dreaming up a play, and it's fun to do! First, think of a story you'd like to tell, either funny or serious. It might even be a story you once dreamed! Choose the characters. Work with friends to write your play. When it's finished, you may wish to perform it. Make puppet characters out of paper bags or old socks. Let your "playdreamers" entertain the rest of the class with your production!

TIPS FOR SPELLING SUCCESS When you write your play, make sure you follow the rules for punctuating dialogue. Remember that in a play, you don't need quotes around the speakers' words. But you *do* need to check that all spelling is correct!

HOW TO FALL ASLEEP

What advice would you give someone who can't fall asleep? Think of some special ways to get sleepy. They may be serious or funny. Then prepare a small booklet titled "How to Fall Asleep." Explain your system, step by step. Add pictures to each page. Later, share your advice with classmates.

Words
to watch for
....
advice
asleep
bedroom
calm
effort
fall
habit
listen
midnight
overnight

TIPS FOR SPELLING SUCCESS After you've finished your writing, invite a classmate to read it. Can your partner find any spelling errors? If so, be sure to correct the misspellings.

BOOKS IN THE CLOUDS

Have you ever heard the expression "in the clouds"? It means "having a daydream." Now you can advertise "dreamy" books you've read by putting them "in the clouds"! Cut out paper clouds from white construction paper. On each cloud, write the name of a book you've enjoyed this year. Also write the author's name and a brief description of the book. But don't give away the ending!

Create a class bulletin board. See what "books in the clouds" your classmates recommend!

TIPS FOR SPELLING SUCCESS As you write your book titles and story descriptions, sound out the words you use. If the spelling looks wrong to you, check it in a dictionary.

HINKY PINKY

You and a partner can have fun playing "Hinky Pinky." Make up a riddle whose answer has two rhyming words, for example: "What kind of bird never breaks the law?" The answer is "a legal eagle." Write out your riddle. See if your partner can guess the answer and write it out. Check his or her spelling to see if it's correct.

TIPS FOR SPELLING SUCCESS Refer to your Spelling Log for lists of science words. Remember to add words to the log that you might want to use again in your writing.

EMERALD FOREST Unit 6 Review • Harcourt Brace School Publishers

Spelling Table

The Spelling Table below has all the sounds that we use to speak the words of English. The first column of the table gives the pronunciation symbol for the sound, such as ō. The second column of the table gives an example of a common word in which this sound appears, such as **open** for the [ō] sound. The third column of the table provides examples of the different ways that the sound

The Sound	In	Is Spelled As	The Sound	In	Is Spelled As
a	add	cat, laugh, plaid	ng	ring	thing, sink, tongue
á	age	game, rain, day, gauge, `steak, weigh, obey, ballet	o	odd	pot, honor
ä	palm	ah, father, dark, heart	ó	open	oh, over, go, oak, grow, toe, though, soul, sew
â(r)	care	dare, fair, prayer, where, bear, their	ô	order	for, more, roar, ball, walk, dawn, fault, broad, ought
b	bat	big, cabin, rabbit	oi	oil	noise, toy
ch	check	chop, march, catch, nature, mention	oo	took	foot, would, wolf, pull
d	dog	dig, bad, ladder, called	o͞o	pool	cool, lose, soup, through, rude, due, fruit, drew, canoe
e	end	egg, met, ready, any, said, says, friend, bury, guess	ou	out	ounce, now, bough
é	equal	she, eat, see, people, key, field, machine, receive, piano, city; here, dear, steer	p	put	pin, cap, happy
			r	run	red, car, hurry, wrist, rhyme
f	fit	five, offer, cough, half, photo	s	see	sit, scene, loss, listen, city, psychology
g	go	gate, bigger, vague, ghost	sh	rush	shoe, sure, ocean, special, machine, mission, lotion, pension, conscience
h	hot	hope, who			
i	it	inch, hit, pretty, been, busy, guitar, damage, women, myth	t	top	tan, kept, better, walked, caught
í	ice	item, fine, pie, high, buy, try, dye, eye, height, island, aisle	th	thin	think, cloth
			t̲h̲	this	these, clothing
j	joy	jump, gem, magic, cage, edge, soldier, graduate, exaggerate	u	up	cut, butter, some, flood, does, young
			û(r)	burn	turn, bird, work, early, journey, herd
k	keep	king, cat, lock, chorus, account	v	very	vote, over, of
l	look	let, ball	w	win	wait, towel
m	move	make, hammer, calm, climb, condemn	y	yet	year, onion
			yo͞o	use	cue, few, youth, view, beautiful
n	nice	new, can, funny, know, gnome, pneumonia	z	zoo	zebra, lazy, buzz, was, scissors
			zh	vision	pleasure, garage, television
			ə	about,	listen, pencil, melon, circus

a•cre [ā′kər] *n.* a measurement of the size of a piece of land: **Farmland is usually divided into** *acres.* [16]

ac•ro•bat [ak′rə•bat′] *n.* a person who is skilled in activities such as tumbling, tightrope walking, or swinging from a trapeze: **A circus often has** *acrobats* **who put on a show for the audience.** [1]

ad•lib [ad′lib′] *v.* **ad libbed, ad libbing.** to make up something to say: **The actor forgot his lines so he had to** *ad lib* **his speech.** [19]

ad•mis•sion [ad•mish′ən] *n.* the amount that it costs to go into a place: **The school charges each person a $3.00** *admission* **to the football game.** [3]

ad•vise [ad•vīz′] *v.* to suggest what a person should do or say; give advice: **The shopping mall will be really crowded today, so I** *advise* **you to get there early.** *syn.* recommend [30]

af•ter•noon [af′tər•noon′] *n.* the part of the day between noon and night; the time after morning: **Our school day starts at 8:00 in the morning and ends at 2:00 in the** *afternoon.* [18]

age [āj] *n.* how old a person or thing is: **Maria and Jill are the same** *age;* **they are both ten years old.** —*v.* to make or grow older: **Some kinds of cheese taste better if they** *age* **for a while.** [7]

a•gent [ā′jənt] *n.* a person who acts for another or others: **A real estate** *agent* **helps people to buy or sell their homes.** [1]

a•gree•ment [ə•grē′mənt] *n.* thinking in the same way: **Mom and Dad are in** *agreement* **that we should sell our old car and buy a new one.** [28]

air•port [âr′pôrt′] *n.* a place where airplanes can land and take off: **We have ten minutes to get to the** *airport* **before our flight leaves.** [26]

al•i•bi [al′ə•bī] *n.* a claim that a person was somewhere else when a crime took place: **The police think he robbed the store, but his** *alibi* **is that he was home in bed at the time.** [20]

al•ley [al′ē] *n.* **1.** a narrow street between or behind buildings: **We keep our garbage cans in the** *alley* **behind our apartment building. 2.** in the game of bowling, the long, narrow wooden path on which the ball is rolled: **You roll the ball down the** *alley* **to knock over the pins.** [20]

al•low [ə•lou′] *v.* to let a person do a certain thing; let something happen: **This school does not** *allow* **students to chew gum in class.** *syn.* permit [14]

a•nem•o•ne [ə•nem′ə•nē] *n.* a sea animal that has a soft, brightly colored body with many long, thin tentacles (little arms): **A sea** *anemone* **gets its name because it looks like a flower growing in the ocean.** [15]

an•i•mal [an′ə•məl] *n.* a living being that is not a plant: **All** *animals* **are different from plants because they can move about on their own and cannot make their own food. The wild** *animals'* **habitats are disappearing quickly.** [25, 21]

an•noy [ə•noi′] *v.* **annoyed, annoying.** bother or disturb a person: **She was trying to watch the movie, and it** *annoyed* **her that two people sitting behind her were talking very loudly.** *syn.* irritate [14]

an•swer [ans′ər] *n.* something said in response to a question: **The** *answer* **to "What is the capital of Texas?" is "Austin."** —*v.* to give a response: **People say "Hello" when they** *answer* **the telephone.** *syn.* reply [24]

an•y•one [en′ē•wun′] *pron.* any person at all: **I thought I heard footsteps, but when I looked out the window there wasn't** *anyone* **there.** [18]

an•y•thing [en′ē•thing′] *pron.* any thing at all: **When you clean your room, make sure you don't leave** *anything* **lying on the floor.** [18]

an•y•way [en′ē•wā′] *adv.* in any case; anyhow: **The weather report said it would be sunny, but he wore his raincoat** *anyway.* *syn.* nevertheless [18]

ap•ply [ə•plī′] *v.* **applied, applying. 1.** to place on a surface; put on: **When I hurt my hand playing baseball, the coach** *applied* **ice to it so that it wouldn't swell up. 2.** to make an official request to get or have something, such as a job or bank loan: **My sister will** *apply* **to the bank for a loan.** [16, 20]

ar•e•a [âr′ē•ə] *n.* **1.** any particular region or section: **The city of Las Vegas, Nevada, is in a desert** *area.* **2.** the measured space within certain limits: **This bedroom is 10 feet by 14 feet, which means it has an** *area* **of 140 square feet.** [10]

a•round [ə•round′] *prep.* on all sides of: **They built a tall fence** *around* **their swimming pool.** —*adv.* in a circle: **On the Spinmaster ride you go** *around* **and** *around* **at a high speed.** [14]

at•ten•tive [ə•ten′tiv] *adj.* paying close attention: **The teacher expects us to be** *attentive* **when she reads us a story.** *syn.* alert [24]

a•void [ə•void′] *v.* to keep away from; keep clear of: **We decided to take Route 15 to** *avoid* **all the heavy traffic on Route 5.** [14]

a•ware [ə•wâr′] *adj.* taking notice of; knowing about: **Are you** *aware* **that you left the front door unlocked last night?** [10]

back•yard [bak′yärd′] *n.* a yard that is in back of a house or other building: **Dad said we can play in the** *backyard* **until he calls us in for dinner.** [18]

ba·con [bā′kən] *n.* a kind of smoked and salted meat that comes from a pig: **People often eat** *bacon* **and eggs for breakfast.** [32]

baf·fle [baf′əl] *v.* **baffled, baffling.** to mix up or confuse: **Some of the difficult math problems** *baffled* **me.** [12]

bak·er [bā′kər] *n.* a person whose work is to make and sell things that are baked in an oven, such as bread, cookies, or cakes: **Mom is going to make Andrew's birthday cake because he doesn't like the ones we buy from the** *baker.* [32]

bal·ance [bal′əns] *v.* **balanced, balancing.** to hold the body in a steady, upright position without leaning or falling: **I** *balanced* **a book on my head while walking across the room.** —*adj.* having the right combination of different things: **She tries to eat a** *balanced* **diet with foods from each of the main food groups.** [1]

bal·loon [bə·lōōn′] *n.* a small rubber bag, usually brightly colored, that can be filled with air or gas: **On my sister's birthday I bought her a red** *balloon* **that bobbed at the end of a string.** [8]

bar·ri·er [bâr′ē·ər] *n.* something that blocks the way or keeps things from moving: **The reef forms a** *barrier* **in the shallow water.** *syn.* obstacle [15]

ba·sic [bā′sik] *adj.* having to do with the simplest or most important part: **You do a lot of different things in the game of soccer, but the** *basic* **thing is kicking the ball.** *syn.* fundamental [32]

bas·ket·ball [bas′kət·bôl′] *n.* **1.** a game played with a large round ball by two teams of five players each: **In the game of** *basketball* **you score points by getting the ball through a ring called a basket. 2.** the ball used in this game: **A** *basketball* **is about 30 inches around.** [18]

basketball

beach [bēch] *n.* the sandy, sloping shore at the edge of an ocean or lake: **There is a** *beach* **near our house where we like to go swimming.** [2]

beau·ti·ful [byōō′ti·fəl] *adj.* pleasing to the eyes or other senses; very pretty: **The rose is a** *beautiful* **flower.** *syn.* lovely [28]

beau·ty [byōō′tē] *n.* **beauties.** the quality of being beautiful to the eyes or other senses: **The state of Hawaii is known for the** *beauty* **of its beaches and mountains.** [20]

be·fore [bi·fôr′] *adj., adv., conj., prep.* at an earlier time: **Timmy has to be home** *before* **dark. Have you seen this movie** *before***? Read over the directions** *before* **you start the test.** [10]

be·gin [bi·gin′] *v.* **began, beginning.** to start something: **I am** *beginning* **to read my new book.** [15]

be·hav·ior [bi·hāv′yər] *n.* the way a person acts: **The police officer's** *behavior* **was calm as he listened to the emergency radio call.** [2]

be·lieve [bi·lēv′] *v.* to accept something as true or real: **I** *believe* **that my sister is a great gymnast.** [12]

ber·ry [ber′ē] *n.* **berries.** a kind of small, sweet fruit: **The farmers' market near our house often sells strawberries and other kinds of** *berries.* [23]

bet·ter [bet′ər] *adj.* of higher quality than something else: **The new dishwasher is** *better* **than our old one; it gets the dishes much cleaner.** [29]

bil·low [bil′ō] *v.* **billowed, billowing.** to wave or swell out, as from the wind: **There was a big fire in the fireplace, and smoke was** *billowing* **out of the chimney.** [25]

blan·ket [blang′kit] *n.* a large covering made of a soft, warm cloth, used on a bed: **She sleeps under a heavy wool** *blanket* **to keep warm.** [30]

board [bôrd] *n.* a flat piece of sawed wood that is longer than it is thick: **After we nail this** *board* **to the doghouse, it will be finished.** [9]

bod·y [bod′ē] *n.* **bodies.** all of a person or animal; the form of a living thing: **Many animals that live in ice and snow, such as the polar bear, have white coloring on their** *bodies.* [23]

bored [bôrd] *adj.* not enjoying what one is doing; not interested: **Mike was** *bored* **with the radio program and tried to find something better.** [9]

bot·tle [bot′əl] *n.* a container with a narrow neck and a mouth that can be closed with a cap, usually used to hold liquids: **Orange juice comes in a** *bottle* **or a carton.** [25]

boun·ti·ful [boun′ti·fəl] *adj.* available in a large quantity: **a** *bountiful* **harvest.** *syn.* plentiful [30]

boy [boi] *n.* a male child: **Jason plays in the** *boys'* **basketball league at the town park.** [21]

a	add	ō	open	th	thin
ā	ace	ô	order	th	this
â(r)	care	oi	oil	zh	vision
ä	palm	ŏŏ	took		
e	end	ōō	pool	ə	a in about
ē	equal	ou	out		e in listen
i	it	u	up		i in pencil
ī	ice	û(r)	burn		o in melon
o	odd	yōō	use		u in circus

bridge   [brij] *n.* a structure built across something to allow travel from one side to the other: **We crossed the *bridge* over the rushing river.** [7]

bring   [bring] *v.* **brought, bringing.** to carry or take along to a place: **I *bring* my lunch from home to eat in school.** [3]

broth·er   [bru*th*´ər] *n.* a male child who has the same parents as another: **I'm not supposed to go into my *brother's* room when he's not there.** [21]

brush   [brush] *n.* a tool having hairs or wires attached to a handle, used for cleaning, for painting, or for arranging the hair: **A painter uses a *brush* to put on paint.** —*v.* to use such a tool: **She *brushes* her hair after she washes it.** [4]

bunch   [bunch] *n.* a number of things of the same kind that are growing or placed together: **a *bunch* of carrots.** [4]

burn   [bûrn] *v.* **burned *or* burnt, burning.** to set on fire or be on fire: **The wood is very dry, and it will *burn* easily.** —*n.* an injury caused by fire or heat: **Stacy got a *burn* on her finger when she touched the hot iron.** [13]

burst   [bûrst] *v.* **burst, bursting.** to break open suddenly: **He blew too much air into the balloon, and it *burst* with a loud bang.** [13]

bus·y   [biz´ē] *adj.* **busier, busiest.** having a lot going on; having a lot of activity: **For many flower shops, Mother's Day is the *busiest* time of the year.** [16]

but·ter   [but´ər] *n.* a food that is a soft, yellowish fat separated from milk: **People often put *butter* on bread and other foods.** [24]

but·ton   [but´ən] *n.* **1.** a hard object that is put onto clothes to hold different parts together: **He took off his necktie and opened the top *button* of his shirt. 2.** a small part that is used to make something work: **To go up in the elevator, push the *button* for the floor you want.** [25]

cal·en·dar   [kal´ən·dər] *n.* a chart on which time is broken down into months, days, and years: **I know that my birthday will be on a Saturday this year because I checked it on the *calendar*.** [24]

calf   [kaf] *n.* **calves.** the young of cattle; a baby cow: **A cow usually has one *calf* each year, but sometimes twin *calves* are born.** [23]

cam·paign   [kam·pān´] *n.* a series of things that a person does to try to win an election: **As part of her *campaign* for mayor, she went all over the city giving speeches.** [3]

cam·pus   [kam´pəs] *n.* the land around a school or college: **The *campus* of Northwestern University is on the shores of Lake Michigan.** [7]

can·di·date   [kan´də·dāt´] *n.* a person who runs for a political office: **Franklin D. Roosevelt was chosen four times by the Democratic Party to be their *candidate* for President.** [3] ♦

♦ **Candidate** goes back to a Latin word meaning "dressed in white." In ancient Rome, people who were running for a political office used to wear special white clothes. The color white was meant to show that the person was honest.

can·non   [kan´ən] *n.* a large gun that shoots a heavy round ball: **The *cannon* at the old fort was used last in a war in the 1800s.** [30]

card   [kärd] *n.* **1.** a small, stiff piece of paper or plastic having something written on it: **a library *card*, a birthday *card*. 2.** a similar object that is part of a set, used in playing games: **"Go Fish" is my little sister's favorite *card* game.** [10]

care·less   [kâr´lis] *adj.* not paying close attention; not taking care: **The dog got out of the yard when Sarah was *careless* and left the gate open.** [28]

cast   [kast] *v.* to throw something: **The fisherman *cast* his line into the water.** [29]

catch   [kach] *v.* **caught, catching. 1.** to take hold of something that is moving and hold or stop it: **to *catch* a baseball. 2.** to get or have in some way: **to *catch* a cold.** [1]

ce·dar   [sē´dər] *n.* a kind of pine tree that is known for its fine wood: **They keep their wool sweaters in a chest made of *cedar*.** [31]

ceil·ing   [sē´ling] *n.* the inside top part of a room: **Every *ceiling* in our house is painted white.** [12]

cel·lar   [sel´ər] *n.* a room or rooms underneath a house, used to store things: **a root *cellar*.** [24]

cent   [sent] *n.* one hundredth part of a dollar; one penny: **"$1.01" is one dollar and one *cent*.** [9]

cen·ter   [sen´tər] *n.* the middle point or part of something: **The *center* of a circle is the same distance from each point on the edge.** [7]

cen·tu·ry   [sen´chə·rē] *n.* **centuries.** a period of one hundred years: **People first landed on the moon in the twentieth *century*.** [23]

cer·e·mo·ny   [ser´ə·mō´nē] *n.* **ceremonies.** a certain action that celebrates something: **When people get married, they have a wedding *ceremony*.** [26]

chan·nel   [chan´əl] *n.* **1.** a number that is used to identify a certain television signal: **Find a *channel* on the television that is broadcasting the evening news. 2.** a way for something to move or pass: **The town dug a *channel* to allow water to flow from the swamp into the river.** [30]

chase [chās] *v.* **chased, chasing.** to go after something in order to get or catch it: **My dog likes** *chasing* **after a stick that I throw to him.** [15]

check [chek] *v.* to look over or test something to see that it is all right: **Before you hand in your paper,** *check* **it over to see if you have made any spelling mistakes.** —*n.* **1.** a mark used to show that something has been noted: **The teacher put a** *check* **next to each correct answer. 2.** a written order to a bank calling for payment of a certain amount of money from a bank account: **Aunt Sue sent Scott a $25** *check* **for his birthday.** [2]

cheer•ful [chir´fəl] *adj.* in a good mood; showing good spirits: **The dentist always smiles and appears to be** *cheerful*. *syn.* happy [28]

chem•i•cal [kem´i•kəl] *n.* a basic substance that things are made of: **Oxygen and hydrogen are** *chemicals* **in the air.** [23]

cher•ry [cher´ē] *n.* **cherries.** a small red fruit that grows on a tree: **Of all the different fruits in fruit cocktail, I like the** *cherries* **best.** [23]

chew [choo] *v.* **chewed, chewing.** to break up or crush food with the teeth so that it can be swallowed: **The meat was very tough and was hard to** *chew*. **I know that** *chewing* **food with my mouth open is not polite.** [4, 15]

chief [chēf] *n.* the person who is the head of a group: **The leader of a Native American tribe is called the** *chief* **of the tribe.** —*adj.* most important; main: **Rice, wheat, corn, and potatoes are the four** *chief* **food crops in the world.** [12]

child [chīld] *n.* **children.** a young person; a boy or girl: **Milk is an important part of a** *child's* **diet. You can pet the animals at the** *children's* **zoo.** [21]

chim•ney [chim´nē] *n.* a pipe or passage through which smoke can move up from a fire: **After we made a fire in our fireplace, I went outside to watch the smoke come out of the** *chimney*. [20]

chimney

choice [chois] *n.* the act of selecting something: **You have a** *choice* **of chocolate cake or apple pie for dessert.** *syns.* selection, preference [14]

chop [chop] *v.* **chopped, chopping.** to cut something with short, quick actions: **to** *chop* **down a tree with a hatchet, to** *chop* **onions with a knife.** [6]

cit•y [sit´ē] *n.* **cities.** a large town where many people live and work: **The largest** *city* **in the United States is New York City.** [7]

clan [klan] *n.* a number of families who are related to a common ancestor: **In Scotland each** *clan* **has its own special plaid color to identify the group.** [26]

class [klas] *n.* a group of students who are in the same grade or are taught together: **I got to know Tim when we sat next to each other in math** *class*. [1]

climb [klīm] *v.* to move upward on something using the hands or feet: **They** *climbed* **to the top of the mountain.** [9]

close [klōz] *v.* to shut something that is open: **Please** *close* **the windows if it starts to rain.** [6]

clown [kloun] *n.* a person whose job is to make people laugh: **The** *clowns* **in the circus wear funny costumes and do silly tricks for the audience.** [14]

coach [kōch] *n.* a person who is in charge of a sports team and who tells the players what to do: **The** *coach* **of my soccer team showed me the right way to kick the ball.** [6]

coin [koin] *n.* a piece of metal, usually flat and round, that is worth a certain amount of money: **In U.S. money the** *coins* **used most often are the penny, nickel, dime, and quarter.** [14]

col•lar [kol´ər] *n.* the part of a piece of clothing that goes around the neck: **He turned up the** *collar* **of his jacket to keep his neck warm.** [24]

col•ored [kul´ərd] *adj.* having color: **I got a box of** *colored* **pencils to use in art class.** [15]

col•or•ful [kul´ər•fəl] *adj.* **1.** full of bright color: **The daisy is a** *colorful* **flower. 2.** interesting or lively: **Brer Rabbit is a** *colorful* **character in the Uncle Remus stories.** [28]

con•sid•er•ate [kən•sid´ər•it] *adj.* caring about the feelings of others; kind: **It was** *considerate* **of you to come to visit me at the hospital when I was sick.** *syn.* thoughtful [30]

con•test [kon´test] *n.* an event that people try to win: **Our teacher had a** *contest* **to see who could guess how many beans there were in the jar on her desk.** [30]

a	add	ō	open	th	thin
ā	ace	ô	order	th	this
â(r)	care	oi	oil	zh	vision
ä	palm	oo	took		
e	end	oo	pool	ə	a in about
ē	equal	ou	out		e in listen
i	it	u	up		i in pencil
ī	ice	û(r)	burn		o in melon
o	odd	yoo	use		u in circus

D

con·tra·dict [kon´trə·dikt´] *v.* **contradicted, contradicting.** to say the opposite: **The lawyer tells me my facts are wrong and keeps** *contradicting* **me.** [24]

cop·per [kop´ər] *n.* a reddish-brown metal that is valuable because it can be used to make things: *Copper* **is often used for electrical wire and for pots and pans for cooking.** [29]

copy [kop´ē] *v.* **copied, copying.** to do or make something that is just like another: **My homework paper got wet, so I** *copied* **what I had written onto a clean sheet of paper.** —*n.* **copies.** something done in this way: **This machine makes** *copies* **of written or printed pages.** [16, 23]

cor·al reef [kôr´əl rēf´] *n.* a hard ridge formed by the bodies of tiny sea animals near the surface of the ocean: **We snorkeled near the** *coral reef* **and saw hundreds of tropical fish.** [15]

cor·ner [kôr´nər] *n.* **1.** the place where two straight lines or surfaces meet: **Write your name in the top right** *corner* **of the paper. 2.** the place where two streets come together: **Our school is on the** *corner* **of Park Avenue and 12th Street.** [24]

coun·try [kun´trē] *n.* **countries. 1.** a large area of land that has its own separate government: **The United States is a** *country* **made up of 50 different states.** *syn.* nation **2.** land away from cities or towns: **a small farm that is far out in the** *country.* [20]

court [kôrt] *n.* **1.** the place where a person is judged for a crime: **The judge requested order in the** *court.* **2.** a marked area on which a game is played: **a tennis** *court.* [10]

cow·er [kou´ər] *v.* **cowered, cowering.** to curl up with fear: **After the loud crack of thunder we found the puppy** *cowering* **under the kitchen table.** [8]

crew [crōō] *n.* a group of people who work together, as on a ship or airplane: **The ocean liner** *Queen Elizabeth 2* **has a** *crew* **of 900 people.** [4]

crowd [croud] *n.* a large group of people close together in one place: **A** *crowd* **of 5,000 people came to the park for the July 4th music show.** —*v.* to press tightly into a small area: **People** *crowded* **around the door waiting to get in.** [14]

cure [kyŏŏr] *v.* to make a person well; bring back to good health: **to** *cure* **someone of a disease.** [13]

curve in a road

curve [kûrv] *n.* a bent line with no straight parts

or angles: **a** *curve* **in a road.** —*v.* to bend or move: **The plant's leaves** *curve* **around the insect.** [13]

cy·clist [sī´klist] *n.* a person who rides a bicycle or motorcycle: **Our state has a law that all** *cyclists* **must wear helmets when riding their bikes.** [4]

dec·ade [dek´ād] *n.* a period of ten years: **The 1950s and the 1960s are famous** *decades.* [23]

deed [dēd] *n.* **1.** something that is done; an action: **Helping the lost child was a good** *deed* **on his part. 2.** a paper that shows who owns a piece of property: **To sell a house, you must have the** *deed* **to prove that you are the owner.** [16]

del·i·cate [del´i·kit] *adj.* not heavy or strong; light and fine: **Those glasses might break if you put them in the dishwasher; they are very** *delicate* **and have to be washed by hand.** *syn.* fragile [6]

de·ny [di·nī´] *v.* **denied, denying.** to say that something is not true: **I** *deny* **that this dog is mine; it just followed me into the store.** [20]

de·scen·dant [di·sen´dənt] *n.* a member of a younger generation of a family; a child or grandchild of an ancestor: **Many people in the state of Minnesota are the** *descendants* **of people who came there from northern Europe in the late 1800s.** [23]

de·tail [dē´tāl´ or di·tāl´] *n.* one certain thing that is a small part of the whole of something: **Lin told us every** *detail* **of her trip to Florida, even what she ate for breakfast every day.** [31]

de·tec·tive [di·tek´tiv] *n.* a police officer or other person whose job is to find out the facts of a crime: **There are many mystery stories about the famous English** *detective,* **Sherlock Holmes.** *syn.* sleuth [12]

de·vice [di·vīs´] *n.* a small tool or object used for a certain purpose: **A jack is a** *device* **used to raise the wheel of a car off the ground.** [19]

dig [dig] *v.* **dug, digging.** to use a tool to break up or turn over dirt; make a hole in the ground: **When Juan is at the beach he loves to spend his time** *digging* **in the sand with a plastic shovel.** —*n.* the act of digging: **No** *digging* **is allowed in the park.** [15]

dis·ap·pear [dis´ə·pēr´] *v.* to go out of view; move out of sight: **I watched the train** *disappear* **in the distance.** *syn.* vanish [19]

dis·com·fort [dis·kum´fərt] *n.* the condition of not being comfortable: **The bus had no air conditioning, which caused the passengers quite a bit of** *discomfort* **on hot days.** [19]

dis·guise [dis•gīz´] *n.* something a person wears to hide who he or she really is: **Carla bought an orange wig to wear with her clown *disguise*.** [12]

doc·tor [dok´tər] *n.* a person who has a license and special training to take care of people who are sick or injured: **A *doctor* who treats children is called a pediatrician.** [24] ♦

♦ **Doctor** first meant "a wise person." The word then came to be used for someone who treats sick people, because of the idea that you need to be very wise to do this.

down·town [doun´toun´] *adv.* in the main part of a city where the stores and office buildings are: **There is a mall near her house, but Grandma still likes to go *downtown* to shop.** [18]

drive [drīv] *v.* **drove, driving, driven. 1.** to direct the movement of a car, truck, or bus: **Chris has a job *driving* a school bus. Mom had *driven* halfway to the office before she realized she'd left her work at home. 2.** to move or cause to go by a strong force: **Gina is *driving* the nail into the board with a hammer.** [15, 24]

drive-in [drīv´in´] *adj.* characteristic of a business where people drive up and are served without getting out of their cars: **a *drive-in* restaurant.** —*n.* an outdoor movie theater. [18]

dry [drī] *v.* **dried, drying.** to take out the water or another liquid from something: **The sun came out after the short rain and quickly *dried* the grass.** —*adj.* not wet: ***Dried* flowers have no moisture in them.** [3]

dust [dust] *n.* dry, very tiny pieces of dirt or other material: **I had not worn my black shoes for two weeks, and there was a layer of *dust* on them.** [4]

du·ty [do͞o´tē] *n.* **duties.** task that is part of a specific job: **At the movie theater, his main *duties* are selling candy and taking tickets.** [32]

ear·ly [ûr´lē] *adv. adj.* **earlier, earliest.** at a time before something else: **to leave *earlier* for school, to take an *earlier* bus.** [16]

earn [ûrn] *v.* to get something in return for what you have done: **Donna is trying to *earn* enough money by babysitting to buy herself a new bike.** [13]

earth [ûrth] *n.* **1.** the planet on which we live: **The *earth* is about 93 million miles away from the sun. 2.** the surface of this planet: **A leaf fell from the tree and dropped slowly to *earth*. 3.** dirt; soil: **rich black *earth* that is good for farming.** [13]

eas·y [ē´zē] *adj.* **easier, easiest.** not hard to do; not difficult: **That was the *easiest* test I took all year; I didn't study and still got 100%.** [16]

edge [ej] *n.* the point at which an object or area ends: **She stood at the *edge* of the canyon and looked down to the river far below.** —*v.* to move gradually: **He was supposed to wait at the back, but he *edged* toward the front of the line.** [7]

eight·een [ā´tēn] *n.* the number that is eight more than ten; 18. [12]

eight·y [ā´tē] *n.* the number that is equal to eight times ten; 80. [12]

ei·ther [ē´thər *or* ī´thər] *adj.* one or the other of two: **The library has two copies of the book; you can borrow *either* one.** —*adv.* also: **I didn't go to the party, and my sister didn't go *either*.** [12]

e·lev·en [i•lev´ən] *n.* the number that is one more than ten; 11. [25]

else [els] *adj. adv.* being another or a different one: **I didn't call you up last night; it must have been somebody *else*.** [2]

e·merge [i•mûrj´] *v.* to come out or become visible: **The movie shows a baby chick as it is born and *emerges* from the egg.** [14]

em·ploy [im•ploi´] *v.* **employed, employing.** to pay someone to do work: **Before he became a teacher he was *employed* in a bookstore.** *syn.* hire [14]

en·dan·gered [in•dān´jərd] *adj.* being in danger of no longer existing: **The manatee is an *endangered* animal.** [10]

end·less [end´lis] *adj.* without any end; going on and on forever: **the *endless* movement of ocean waves against the shore.** [28]

en·vi·ron·ment [in•vī´rə•mənt *or* in•vī´rən•mənt] *n.* the place where something lives, its surroundings: **The cactus thrives in a dry desert *environment*.** *syn.* conditions [13]

e·qual [ē´kwəl] *adj.* being the same in amount or value as something else: **One hundred cents is *equal* to one dollar.** [31]

eve·ry·bod·y [ev´rē•bud´ē *or* ev´rē•bod´ē] *pron.* every person: **This year *everybody* in our family was home for Thanksgiving.** [26]

eve·ry·one [ev´rē•wun´] *pron.* every person: **I know the name of *everyone* who lives on my street.** [26]

a	add	ō	open	th	thin
ā	ace	ô	order	th	this
â(r)	care	oi	oil	zh	vision
ä	palm	o͝o	took		
e	end	o͞o	pool	ə	a in about
ē	equal	ou	out		e in listen
i	it	u	up		i in pencil
ī	ice	û(r)	burn		o in melon
o	odd	yo͞o	use		u in circus

eve·ry·thing [ev´rē·thing´] *pron.* all things: **When we moved we took** *everything* **we owned.** [26]

ex·am·ple [ig·zam´pəl] *n.* one of a group of things, used to show what the others are like: **Orange is an** *example* **of a warm color.** *syn.* sample [25]

eye [ī] *n.* the part of the body that sees: **The** *eye* **cannot see anything in total darkness.** [3]

fair [fâr] *adj.* **1.** doing things in the right way: **A** *fair* **baseball umpire never calls plays to favor one team. 2.** clear and sunny. *fair* **weather. 3.** not very good or very bad: **She was a good pitcher but only a** *fair* **catcher.** [10]

fam·i·ly [fam´lē *or* fam´ə·lē] *n.* **families.** a mother and father and their children; a group of people with common ancestors; the members of a household: **I took those pictures during our** *family's* **vacation last summer.** [21]

fa·ther [fä´thər] *n.* the male parent of a child: **His middle name is Robert, which is his** *father's* **first name.** [21]

fe·male [fē´māl] *n.* a woman or girl: **Any person, male or** *female,* **can apply for this job.** —*adj.* an animal of the sex that gives birth: **The** *female* **lion, not the male, hunts food for her young.** [31]

fe·ver [fē´vər] *n.* a body temperature that is higher than the normal temperature: **Often a person who is sick will have a** *fever.* [31]

few [fyo͞o] *adj.* being a small number: **It was a cold, wet day and there were only a** *few* **people at the beach.** [4]

field [fēld] *n.* a large, open piece of land with few or no trees: **The farmer planted wheat in the** *field.* [12]

fifth [fifth] *adj.* next after the fourth. [3]

fi·nal·ly [fī´nə·lē] *adv.* at last, at the end: **We** *finally* **finished our chores.** [13]

find [fīnd] *v.* **found, finding.** to locate: **I looked all over for my book and finally** *found* **it under my bed.** [14]

fire·fight·er [fīr´fī´tər] *n.* a person whose job is to put out or stop fires: **A** *firefighter* **came to our school to tell us about what we can do to keep our homes safe from fire.** [26] ♦

♦ **Firefighter** is a fairly new word. In the past when only men had this job, the word used was *fireman.* Now that many women also do this job, the word *firefighter* is used instead.

---

fire·place [fīr´plās´] *n.* an open place at the bottom of a chimney that holds a fire: **In the days of log cabins, the fire in the** *fireplace* **was the main way to heat the house.** [26]

float [flōt] *v.* to rest on top of a liquid without sinking: **A piece of wood will** *float* **on water because of the air bubbles trapped inside the wood.** [6]

flood [flud] *n.* a very large flow of water onto land that is usually dry: **There was water a foot deep in our basement during last year's** *flood.* [18]

flow [flō] *v.* to move in a smooth, steady way, as moving water does: **Which way does the Hudson River** *flow*? [6]

fo·cus [fō´kəs] *v.* to fix the mind on something: **I don't put the TV on while I'm studying so that I can** *focus* **on what I am doing.** *syn.* concentrate [31]

fore·close [fôr´klōz´] *v.* to reclaim property when payments have not been made: **If a person does not pay his or her mortgage to the bank, the bank can** *foreclose* **on the property and take over as owner of the house.** [16]

for·est [fôr´ist] *n.* a large area with many trees: **Our class took a nature hike in the** *forest.* [14]

for·ward [fôr´wərd] *adj. adv.* at or to the front: **You put the car in Reverse to go backward and in Drive to go** *forward.* [30]

foul [foul] *n.* a baseball that is hit outside the first- or third-base line: **The baseball player hit three** *fouls* **before he hit a home run.** [31]

frame [frām] *v.* **framed, framing.** to cause someone to look guilty of committing a crime: **Louis put a stolen camera in Jim's house and** *framed* **Jim.** [20]

free [frē] *adj.* **1.** not under anyone else's control: **The U.S. is a** *free* **country where the people can choose their own leaders. 2.** costing nothing: **The store gave me a** *free* **balloon on my birthday.** [2]

fried [frīd] *adj.* cooked in hot fat or oil: *Fried* **potatoes are a popular food in many countries.** [3]

friend [frend] *n.* a person who is known and liked by another person: **Susan is my best** *friend.* [12]

fun·ny [fun´ē] *adj.* **funnier, funniest. 1.** making someone laugh: **I think** *Home Alone* **is the** *funniest* **movie I've ever seen.** *syn.* amusing **2.** odd or unusual; strange: **The car is making a** *funny* **noise; maybe something's wrong with the engine.** [16, 20]

fur [fûr] *n.* the soft, hairy covering of certain animals: **Animals that live in cold places, such as the polar bear, usually have very thick** *fur.* [13]

fur·nace [fûr´nis] *n.* a large chamber where fuel is burned to produce heat: **Steel is made by melting metal in huge** *furnaces.* [25]

fu·ry [fyŏŏr´ē] *n.* **furies.** great anger: **Storm winds tore the roof to the house off as if in a** *fury.* [8]

fu·ture [fyōō´chər] *n.* the time that is yet to come: **Her job does not pay very well, and she hopes to get a better job in the near** *future.* [32]

gau·cho [gou´chō] *n.* a name for the cowboys of the South American plains: **The** *gauchos* **raised cattle in the early days of Argentina.** [32]

gen·er·a·tion [jen´ə·rā´shən] *n.* all the people born about the same time: **The people in my grandfather's** *generation* **listened to big band music.** [23]

gift [gift] *n.* **1.** something that is given: **At Tina's birthday party she got a** *gift* **from each of her friends.** *syn.* present **2.** a special talent or skill: **a** *gift* **for music, a** *gift* **for playing chess.** [3]

gill [gil] *n.* the body part that fish and other such water animals use to breathe: **Fish use their** *gills* **to take in oxygen from the water.** [29]

glad [glad] *adj.* feeling good about something; pleased, happy: **My friend was sick last week, and I am** *glad* **that she is feeling better now.** [1]

glis·ten [glis´ən] *v.* **glistened, glistening.** to shine: **The water of the lake** *glistened* **in the bright moonlight.** *syns.* sparkle, glimmer [6]

gold [gōld] *n.* a soft yellowish metal that is very valuable: **Rings and jewelry are often made of** *gold* **because it is both strong and beautiful.** [6]

gold·en [gōl´dən] *adj.* **1.** made of gold: **a** *golden* **necklace. 2.** having the color of gold; bright yellow: *golden* **hair.** [25]

good-bye [gŏŏd·bī´] *interj.* a word that we say when we go away from someone: **People also say** *"good-bye"* **when they stop talking to someone on the phone.** [18]

goods [gŏŏdz] *n.* things that can be bought and sold: **In the days before airplanes,** *goods* **were sent from Europe to America by ship.** [8]

grade [grād] *n.* **1.** one level of study in school: **first** *grade,* **sixth** *grade.* **2.** one step in a system of rank or worth: **The highest** *grade* **you can get in this course is A+.** [1]

grad·u·a·tion [graj´ōō·ā´shən] *n.* the successful finishing of one's studies in a school or college: **At my older sister's high school** *graduation,* **each student received a diploma from the principal.** [7]

gram·mar [gram´ər] *n.* rules for using the words of a language. [30]

gray [grā] *adj.* a color that is a mixture of black and white: **Most wolves have a** *gray* **color.** [1]

great [grāt] *adj.* very, very good; outstanding in some way: **Michael Jordan is one of the** *great* **basketball players in the history of the game.** *syn.* excellent [1]

ground [ground] *n.* the solid surface of the earth: **At the park we sat right down on the** *ground* **to eat our lunch.** [14]

guess [ges] *v.* to give an answer without knowing enough to be sure: **I don't know how much that car costs; I would** *guess* **about $20,000.** [2]

gym [jim] *n.* a large room or building used for sports such as basketball and volleyball and for physical education classes: **The word** *gym* **is short for** *gymnasium.* [7]

hair [hâr] *n.* long, very thin parts that grow on the head and other parts of the body: **Cathy and her mom both have blonde** *hair.* [10]

hang [hang] *v.* **hung, hanging.** put up in a place: **All her clothes were** *hung* **carefully in the closet.** [4]

hap·pen [hap´ən] *v.* **happened, happening.** to take place: **I know that the accident** *happened* **at 4:00, because I looked at the clock when I heard the crash.** *syn.* occur [15]

hap·pi·ness [hap´ē·nis] *n.* being pleased or happy: **When Jennie got a puppy for her birthday, you could see the** *happiness* **all over her face.** [28]

harbor

har·bor [här´bər] *n.* a sheltered place on the coast of an ocean, lake, or river, where ships can anchor or be safe during a storm: **San Diego has a large** *harbor* **where many Navy ships are kept.** [24]

a	add	ō	open	th	thin
ā	ace	ô	order	th	this
â(r)	care	oi	oil	zh	vision
ä	palm	ŏŏ	took		
e	end	ōō	pool	ə	a in about
ē	equal	ou	out		e in listen
i	it	u	up		i in pencil
ī	ice	û(r)	burn		o in melon
o	odd	yōō	use		u in circus

haze   [hāz] *n.* dust particles in the air: **The** *haze* **made it difficult to see the distant buildings.** [28]

hear   [hēr] *v.* **heard** [hûrd], **hearing.** to sense with the ears: **Could you say that again—I don't think I** *heard* **you correctly.** [9]

heav•y   [hev´ē] *adj.* **heavier, heaviest.** having great weight: **In winter people wear** *heavier* **clothes than they do in summer. The** *heaviest* **box in my closet is full of books.** [16]

height   [hīt] *n.* the distance from the bottom of an object to its top: **The giraffe can reach a** *height* **of 18 feet.** [12]

help•ful   [help´fəl] *adj.* giving help: **Our librarian is always** *helpful* **when I want to find a book.** [28]

help•less   [help´lis] *adj.* not having strength or power; not able to do things: **Newborn babies are almost** *helpless,* **and they need a lot of care.** [28]

herd   [hûrd] *n.* a large number of animals that are together in one group: **a** *herd* **of cattle, a** *herd* **of wild buffalo.** [9]

hide   [hīd] *v.* **hid, hidden.** to place out of sight, to cover: **The entrance to the cave was** *hidden* **by bushes.** *syn.* conceal —*adj.* not easily known or seen: *hidden* **information.** *syn.* secret [30]

hock•ey   [hok´ē] *n.* a game played on ice by two teams of six skaters, using curved wooden sticks: **In** *hockey,* **you try to hit a rubber disk called a puck into the other team's goal.** [20]

hole   [hōl] *n.* an opening or hollow place in something: **a** *hole* **in the ground, an old shirt with a** *hole* **in one elbow.** [9]

home run   [hōm´ run´] *n.* in baseball, a hit that travels far enough to allow the batter to go around all the bases and score a run: **He hit the ball over the left-field fence for a** *home run.* [26]

hook   [hŏŏk] *n.* a sharply curved object, sometimes with a point at one end, used to catch or hold things: **a** *hook* **for catching fish, a** *hook* **in a closet to hang clothes on.** [8]

hope•less   [hōp´lis] *adj.* without hope: **He had lost all his money, and things seemed** *hopeless.* [28]

how•ev•er   [hou•ev´ər] *conj.* even so; in any case: **Dan didn't want to go to the play;** *however,* **he enjoyed it once he got there.** *syn.* nevertheless [18]

hu•mor   [hyōō´mər] *n.* the quality of being funny or amusing: **There is a lot of** *humor* **in that book, and I laughed out loud as I read it.** [32]

hur•ry   [hûr´ē] *v.* **hurried, hurrying.** to move quickly: **The bus leaves in ten minutes, so we have to** *hurry.* **She saw that her class was about to start and** *hurried* **into the room.** *syn.* rush [16, 20]

hy•drant   [hī´drənt] *n.* a water outlet to which hoses can be attached: **A** *hydrant* **is used by firefighters to get water from a main water pipe.** [28]

ice cream   [īs´• krēm´] *n.* a sweet frozen food that people eat for dessert: **vanilla** *ice cream.* [26]

im•me•di•ate•ly   [i•mē´dē•it•lē] *adv.* right away; at once: **When he heard the noise, he** *immediately* **went to see what it was.** [13]

in•ning   [in´ing] *n.* the time at bat it takes each baseball team to make three outs: **A big-league game is nine** *innings* **long, but a Little League game is six** *innings.* [31]

in•no•cent   [in´ə•sənt] *adj.* not guilty of doing something wrong: **He is** *innocent* **of the crime and should not be arrested.** [20]

in•struc•tor   [in•struk´tər] *n.* a person who teaches: **I learned to swim from the swimming** *instructor* **at camp.** *syn.* teacher [7]

in•ten•si•ty   [in•ten´si•tē] *n.* the concentrated strength or force of something: **Dawn wore a straw hat to protect her from the** *intensity* **of the sun's rays.** [8]

in•to   [in´tōō] *prep.* toward the inside of: **Put the soup mix** *into* **a pot and add a can of water.** [8]

join   [join] *v.* **1.** to bring or come together: **The pieces of a jigsaw puzzle** *join* **each other.** *syn.* connect **2.** to become a part of: **to** *join* **a club, to** *join* **the Girl Scouts.** [14]

jour•ney   [jûr´nē] *n.* a trip, especially a long one: **The Pilgrims made their** *journey* **to America in a small sailing ship.** [20]

judge   [juj] *n.* the person who is in charge of cases in a court of law: **The** *judge* **told the jury how the law applied to their case.** [7]

ken•nel   [ken´əl] *n.* a place to keep a dog: **Our dog Barkis stayed at the** *kennel* **while we were away on vacation.** [7]

key   [kē] *n.* an object that is used to open a lock: **There are two** *keys* **to our house, one for the front door and one for the back.** [23]

knife [nīf] *n.* **knives.** a sharp tool used to cut food: **Forks go on the left of the plate, and *knives* and spoons go on the right.** [23]

knock [nok] *v.* **knocked, knocking.** to make a short, loud noise: **The bell didn't work, so he *knocked* on the door.** [6]

know [nō] *v.* **knew, knowing.** to have fixed in the mind: **I already *knew* his phone number, so I didn't have to look in the book. She doesn't think she can do a report on electricity without *knowing* a lot more about the subject.** [4, 6]

la·bor [lā´bər] *n.* the act of doing work, especially hard physical work: **It takes hours of *labor* in the kitchen to run that restaurant successfully.** [24]

lad·der [lad´ər] *n.* a device used for climbing up and down, made of two long side pieces joined by a series of crosspieces: **The painter stood on a *ladder* to paint the ceiling.** [29]

las·so [las´ō *or* las´ōō] *n.* a long rope with a loop at one end that can be tightened: **A cowboy can use a *lasso* to catch a runaway steer.** [32]

la·va [lä´və] *n.* the hot liquid rock that flows out from an active volcano: **Lava comes from deep in the earth where the heat is very great.** [18]

leaf [lēf] *n.* **leaves.** the green part of a tree or other plant, growing out from the stem: **The *leaves* of the maple tree turn orange-red in the fall.** [23]

learn [lûrn] *v.* to gain knowledge or skill by study or experience: **to *learn* math in school, to *learn* to speak French, to *learn* how to ride a bike.** [13]

least [lēst] *adj. adv. n.* the smallest: **One dollar is the *least* you can give. Of all my classes, I like math best and English *least*.** [2]

le·gal [lē´gəl] *adj.* according to the law: **In this state it is not *legal* to drive a car until you are sixteen years old.** *syn.* lawful [31]

lem·on [lem´ən] *n.* an oval citrus fruit with yellow thick skin and juicy sour pulp: **A *lemon* has a very sour taste.** [25]

les·son [les´ən] *n.* something to be learned; a part of a course of study: **There will be a science test after we do the third *lesson* in our book.** [30]

let·ter [let´ər] *n.* **1.** a written message sent from one person to another, usually placed in an envelope and delivered by mail: **I just got a *letter* from my cousin in Ohio. 2.** one of a set of characters that are used for writing: **'A' is the first *letter* in the English alphabet.** [24]

lightning

light·ning [līt´ning] *n.* a sudden, bright flash of light in the sky caused by electricity in the air: **The *lightning* streaked across the black sky.** [8]

lis·ten [lis´ən] *v.* to try to hear something: **to *listen* to what a teacher says, to *listen* to a program on the radio.** [25]

lock [lok] *n.* a device that is used to hold something closed or in place and that is usually opened with a key: **Jim puts a *lock* on his bike when he parks it at school. —*v.* to fasten something in this way: **Be sure to *lock* the door when you go out.** [6]

log·i·cal [loj´i·kəl] *adj.* done in a way that is orderly or makes sense: **If you think it's going to rain, it's *logical* to wear a raincoat.** *syn.* sensible [12]

loose [lōōs] *adj. adv.* free, not fastened or held tight: **The dog was supposed to be on his leash, but he got *loose* and ran after the cat.** [8]

loy·al [loi´əl] *adj.* being true to something: **She is always *loyal* to her friends and doesn't criticize them to other people.** *syn.* faithful [14]

luck [luk] *n.* **1.** good fortune; success: **We wished Tess *luck* in her new job. 2.** the way things happen by chance, either good or bad: **It was bad *luck* that it rained the day of our picnic.** *syn.* fate [4]

lum·ber [lum´bər] *n.* wood that is cut into boards or planks: **The builder ordered some *lumber* to use in building the house.** *v.* **lumbered, lumbering.** to move in a slow, heavy way: **When it saw us, the bear turned and *lumbered* slowly back into the woods.** [21, 29]

a	add	ō	open	th	thin
ā	ace	ô	order	th	this
â(r)	care	oi	oil	zh	vision
ä	palm	ŏŏ	took		
e	end	ōō	pool	ə	a in about
ē	equal	ou	out		e in listen
i	it	u	up		i in pencil
ī	ice	û(r)	burn		o in melon
o	odd	yōō	use		u in circus

M

mail [māl] *n.* letters and packages sent from one place to another by a government system: **On her birthday, Kelly got a present in the *mail* from her aunt in Chicago.** [1]

ma·jor [mā´jər] *adj.* greater in number or value: **Transportation to the art festival for our class is a *major* problem.** [32]

man·ner [man´ər] *n.* a certain way of doing things or of acting: **The school crossing guard had a very friendly *manner* and always had a nice word to say to the students.** [24]

mar·ket [mär´kit] *n.* a public place where things are bought and sold, especially things to eat: **We buy fresh fruits and vegetables at the farmers' *market* every Saturday morning.** [29]

mas·ter [mas´tər] *n.* a person who directs or controls others: **The dog was very well trained, and it followed all the commands of its *master*.** [29]

mat·ter [mat´ər] *n.* anything that takes up space and has weight: **Air and water are forms of *matter*. —*v.* to make a difference; be important: **We can have either fish or chicken for dinner; it doesn't *matter* to me.** [24]

mean [mēn] *adj.* not nice or kind: **Making fun of her hair was a *mean* thing for him to do.** *syn.* cruel —*v.* to have a certain idea: **The English word *five* and the Spanish word *cinco* both *mean* the same thing, "5."** [2]

mem·ber [mem´bər] *n.* a person who belongs to a certain group: **a *member* of a club, a *member* of the team.** [29]

mem·o·ry [mem´rē *or* mem´ə·rē] *n.* memories. something that is remembered: **My favorite *memory* is of my first time on roller skates. The "Little House" books are written from the author's *memories* of her life as a little girl.** [2, 23]

men [men] *n.* a group of males: **Dan Jansen won many championships in *men's* speed skating.** [21]

mind [mīnd] *n.* the part of a person that thinks and feels: **She has a very good *mind* and can learn new things quickly.** *syn.* intelligence —*v.* to obey, pay attention to: **Jed had to *mind* his big sister while his mother was at the store.** [3]

mine [mīn] *pron.* belonging to me; my own: **That book is *mine*; there's my name on the inside of the cover. —*n.* a hole or tunnel dug in the earth to take out minerals: **a gold *mine*, a coal *mine*.** [3]

mi·nor [mī´nər] *adj.* not large or important: **The accident caused only *minor* damage because both cars were going so slowly.** [31]

mi·nus [mī´nəs] *prep.* without a certain amount: **The answer to "six *minus* four" is "two."** [31]

mis·be·have [mis´bē·hāv´] *v.* to behave in the wrong way; act badly: **If you *misbehave*, the teacher will write your name on the board.** [19]

mis·chief [mis´chif] *n.* actions that cause harm: **Play safely at the pool; don't splash swimmers and get into *mischief*.** [16]

mis·spell [mis·spel´] *v.* misspelled, misspelling. to spell a word in the wrong way; spell incorrectly: **I *misspelled* the word *friend* and wrote *freind* instead.** [19]

mis·take [mis·tāk´] *n.* something that is done wrong: **He made a *mistake* in adding up the numbers and put 136 when the right answer was 139.** *syn.* error [19]

mis·un·der·stand [mis´un·dər·stand´] *v.* misunderstood, misunderstanding. to interpret something in the wrong way: **He asked her to repeat what she had said to be sure that he did not *misunderstand* her.** [19]

mon·o·tone [mon´ə·tōn´] *n.* a way of speaking in a constant tone of voice, with no high or low tones: **The actor spoke in a *monotone* and bored the audience.** [19]

morn·ing [môr´ning] *n.* the early part of the day, after night and before afternoon: **Breakfast is a meal people eat in the *morning*.** [10]

moth·er [muth´ər] *n.* the female parent of a child: **Michelle borrowed her *mother's* sweater to wear to the party.** [21]

mo·tion [mō´shən] *n.* 1. the act of moving: **The strong *motion* of the waves made the small boat rock back and forth.** *syn.* movement 2. a suggestion to be voted upon by a special group or assembly: **I support the *motion* to plant new trees in our neighborhood.** [31]

mo·tor [mō´tər] *n.* a machine that makes something move: **The blades of the food processor are turned by a small electric *motor*.** [24]

mo·tor·cy·cle [mō´tər·sī´kəl] *n.* a two-wheeled motor vehicle that is something like a bicycle but is larger and heavier: **A *motorcycle* is powered by a gasoline engine.** [26]

move [mo͞ov] *v.* moved, moving. to go or cause to go from one place to another: **It was too hot to sit in the sun, so he *moved* into the shade.** [15]

move·ment [mo͞ov´mənt] *n.* an organized group of activities with a specific goal: **I joined the *movement* to save the whales.** [28]

mul·ti·ply [mul´ti·plī] *v.* multiplied, multiplying. 1. to increase in number: **The plants *multiply* each year because of the rich soil. 2. to add a number to itself a certain number of times: **Three *multiplied* by four is twelve.** [16, 20]

mus•cle [mus´əl] *n.* a special body tissue that can stretch or tighten to cause movement: **Tyler has been lifting weights and has built up strong *muscles* in his arms.** [4] ♦

♦ **Muscle** actually comes from a very old word meaning "a little mouse." The muscles can be seen moving under the skin, and people thought this looked something like the way a "little mouse" would move. In more modern times, the small device that controls the cursor on a computer has also come to be called a "mouse." Here also the idea is that it looks and moves something like a mouse.

---

mu•sic [myoo´zik] *n.* a special arrangement of sounds produced by the voice or an instrument: **The song "America the Beautiful" is a famous piece of *music*.** [32]

na•tion [nā´shən] *n.* a group of people who have a common language, history, and way of life and who live in one place under one government: **the *nation* of Japan.** *syn.* country [32]

na•tion•al [nash´nəl *or* nash´ə•nəl] *adj.* having to do with an entire nation: **The President of the United States is chosen in a *national* election.** [25]

na•tive [nā´tiv] *n.* a person who was born in a certain place: **Charlie Chaplin became a famous motion picture actor in the United States, but he was a *native* of England.** —*adj.* belonging to a person or area by birth: **The *native* language of the Netherlands is Dutch.** [32]

nat•u•ral [nach´ə•rəl] *adj.* **1.** found in nature; not made by humans: **Cotton is a *natural* fabric that comes from a plant; polyester is an artificial fabric made from chemicals. 2.** born in a person; not taught: **Newborn babies have a *natural* habit of holding on tight to the things they touch.** [25]

na•ture [nā´chər] *n.* **1.** the whole world of living things: **The land, the oceans, the animals, and the plants are all part of *nature*. 2.** the basic qualities of something that make it what it is: **It is the *nature* of a wolf to hunt other animals.** [32]

near•by [nir´bī´] *adj. adv.* close at hand; near: **The children go to a school *nearby* their homes.** [26]

neigh•bor [nā´bər] *n.* a person who lives near someone else: **People whose houses are on the same street are *neighbors*.** [12]

nei•ther [nē´thər *or* nī´thər] *adj. pron. conj.* not either; not one nor the other: **We don't shop at that store because my dad doesn't like it and *neither* does my mom.** [12]

nest [nest] *n.* a place that birds use to lay their eggs and raise their young: **A pair of robins built a *nest* in the oak tree by my window.** [2]

nev•er•the•less [nev´ər•thə•les´] *conj.* in spite of that; anyway: **I don't agree with the idea; *nevertheless,* I'm willing to hear the reasons in favor of it.** *syn.* however [26]

news•pa•per [nooz´pā´pər] *n.* a collection of news stories and other things to read, printed on separate sheets of paper folded together: **Our town *newspaper* has an issue every day of the week.** [18]

next [nekst] *adv. adj.* coming or being near in time or place: **She sat in the empty seat *next* to her friend. We'll have to hurry if we want to see the movie; the *next* show starts in half an hour.** [2]

no•bod•y [nō´bud´ē *or* nō´bod´ē] *pron.* no person; no one: **I let the phone ring ten times, but *nobody* answered.** [18]

noise [noiz] *n.* a sound that can be heard, especially a loud or disturbing sound: **An airplane that is taking off makes a lot of *noise*.** [14]

note•book [nōt´book´] *n.* a book of blank pieces of paper, used for writing notes: **Dave wrote down the math problem in his *notebook*.** [18]

no•tice [nō´tis] *v.* to see or become aware of something: **Did you *notice* that Tara just got a new haircut?** —*n.* a statement in writing: **They got a *notice* in the mail about a town meeting.** [31]

no•where [nō´wâr´ *or* nō´hwâr´] *adv.* not anywhere; in no place: **There was *nowhere* to sit, and so we had to stand.** [26]

odd [od] *adj.* not normal or usual: **Roast beef and jelly is an *odd* combination of foods for a sandwich.** *syn.* strange [6]

oft•en [of´ən *or* of´tən] *adv.* many times: **The twins look very much alike, and people *often* get them mixed up.** *syn.* frequently [25]

---

a	add	ō	open	th	thin
ā	ace	ô	order	th	this
â(r)	care	oi	oil	zh	vision
ä	palm	oo	took		
e	end	oo	pool	ə	a in about
ē	equal	ou	out		e in listen
i	it	u	up		i in pencil
ī	ice	û(r)	burn		o in melon
o	odd	yoo	use		u in circus

once   [wuns]   *adv.* **1.** only one time: **That TV show is on *once* a week. 2.** at one time: **All this land was *once* covered with trees.** —*conj.* as soon as: **He can go out to play *once* he finishes his homework.** [7]

orange tree

or•ange   [ôr´inj *or* or´inj] *n.* **1.** a round, juicy, sweet citrus fruit with thick orange skin: **I sometimes peel an *orange* for breakfast. 2.** the color of this fruit: **The color *orange* is a mixture of yellow and red.** [7]

or•di•nar•y   [ôr´di•när´ē] *adj.* not special or different; usual or normal: **This is *ordinary* writing paper that you can buy in any store.** [6]

o•ver•take   [ō´vər•tāk´] *v.* **overtook, overtaking.** to catch up with from behind: **She was behind at the start of the race, but she *overtook* the other runners and went on to win.** [4]

ox•y•gen   [ok´sə•gin] *n.* a gas that is an important part of the air we breathe: **Animals need *oxygen* to stay alive.** [14]

page   [pāj] *n.* one side of a sheet of paper in a book, newspaper, or the like: **The title *page* of a book tells the name of the book and who wrote it.** [7]

pair   [pâr] *n.* a set of two things that are alike in some way: **a *pair* of socks, a *pair* of sneakers.** [9]

pale   [pāl] *adj.* not having much color or brightness: **She must be sick; her face looks very *pale*.** [6]

pam•pas   [pam´pəz] *n.* a name for the flat grasslands of South America: **Cattle are raised on the *pampas* of central Argentina.** [32]

pa•per   [pā´pər] *n.* a common material used for writing, for printing books, for wrapping things, and for many other purposes: **You can make *paper* from wood pulp, rags, or certain grasses.** [24]

pare   [pâr] *n.* to cut off the skin or outer covering of something: **to *pare* an apple.** *syn.* peel [9]

par•ent   [pâr´ənt] *n.* a father or mother: **My**

parents have been married for fifteen years. **Mrs. Long and her brothers are planning a party for their *parents'* fiftieth wedding anniversary.** [10, 21]

par•ty   [pär´tē] *n.* **parties.** a time when people get together to have fun or to celebrate something: **Two boys in my class will celebrate their birthdays with *parties* this month.** [23]

pa•tient   [pā´shənt] *adj.* able to wait for something without complaining or getting angry: **The *patient* customers waited in line to pay for their purchases.** —*n.* a person who is treated by a doctor: **That hospital has enough beds to take care of 200 *patients*.** [32]

pay•ment   [pā´mənt] *n.* the act of paying: **The *payment* for the rent is due the first week of every month.** [28]

peace   [pēs] *n.* a time when there is no fighting; a time without war: **There has been *peace* between the United States and England since they fought the War of 1812.** [9]

pear   [pâr] *n.* a sweet, juicy fruit with a thin yellow or brownish skin: **The *pear* grows on trees in warm areas all over the world.** [9]

ped•al   [ped´əl] *v.* to push with your feet the device that causes a bicycle to move: **to *pedal* a bicycle.** [4]

peer   [pēr] *v.* **peered, peering.** to look closely at something: **He *peered* at the road sign through the darkness, trying to read the letters.** [28]

pen•cil   [pen´səl] *n.* a thin stick with a point at one end, used to write or draw: **A *pencil* is usually made of wood with a graphite core.** [7]

pen•ny   [pen´ē] *n.* **pennies.** a coin that is worth one cent: **One hundred *pennies* are worth the same as one dollar bill.** [23]

peo•ple   [pē´pəl] *n.* a group of human beings; persons: **The Bill of Rights states the American *people's* right to freedom of speech.** [21]

pic•nic   [pik´nik] *n.* a meal eaten outdoors: **Our family always has a *picnic* in the park on July Fourth, with hot dogs and hamburgers.** [29]

piece   [pēs] *n.* an item of some kind; one of a group or set: **a *piece* of thread, a *piece* of paper.** [9]

pi•lot   [pī´lət] *n.* the person who operates an airplane: **The *pilot* guided the plane down to the ground for a landing.** [31] ◆

◆ **Pilot** comes from a word that meant the oar used to steer a boat. *Pilot* used to mean a person who guides a ship. After airplanes were invented, it was used for the person who guides a plane.

pi•rate [pī´rət] *n.* a person who robs ships at sea: **Blackbeard was a famous *pirate* who operated off the coast of North Carolina during the 1700s.** [32]

place [plās] *n.* a certain spot or area: **She drove around the parking lot looking for a *place* to park.** *syn.* location —*v.* to put in a certain spot: **If you *place* your hand on your chest, you can feel your heart beating.** [1]

plains [plānz] *n.* a large flat area of land, usually with grass and few or no trees: **Wheat is grown in the *plains* of the central United States.** [9]

plan [plan] *v.* to think ahead about how to do something: **Both girls *plan* to go on to college after they finish high school.** —*n.* a way to do something: **The President said that he had a *plan* to cut taxes in this country.** [1]

plane [plān] *n.* a vehicle that flies through the air; an airplane: **I hear *planes* land and take off at the airport all day.** [9]

plant [plant] *n.* a living thing, such as a flower, bush, or tree, that is not an animal: **A *plant* makes its own food and cannot move about on its own.** —*v.* to place something in the ground so that it can take root and grow: **This spring we are going to *plant* rose bushes along the fence.** [1]

plas•tic [plas´tik] *n.* a manufactured material that can be shaped to form various products: **Manufacturers use *plastic* to make many different things, such as toys, bags, and bottles.** [30]

play [plā] *v.* to do something to have fun: **After school Mike usually *plays* in the backyard with his friend Tommy.** —*n.* a story that is performed on a stage for an audience: **William Shakespeare wrote many *plays* that are still popular today.** [23]

plen•ty [plen´tē] *n.* more than enough of something; a lot: **We have *plenty* of food on hand in case any extra people come to the party.** *syn.* abundance [20]

plot [plot] *n.* **1.** the story of a book, movie, or play: **The book *Treasure Island* has an exciting *plot* in which a young boy tries to escape from a gang of pirates. 2.** a secret plan to do something wrong: **a *plot* to rob a bank.** [6]

po•lar [pō´lər] *adj.* being or living near the North or South Pole: **The *polar* bear has a thick white fur that protects it from the bitter cold.** [31]

po•lice [pə•lēs´] *n.* a government force whose job is to see that people obey the law: **The *police* patrol our neighborhood to prevent crime.** [7]

pol•len [pol´ən] *n.* a powder produced by flowering plants that enables seeds to grow: **Birds, insects, and wind carry *pollen* from one plant to another.** [14]

Shetland pony

po•ny [pō´nē] *n.* **ponies.** a type of small horse: **The girls all wanted to take a ride on the *pony* at the farm.** [20]

pos•si•ble [pos´i•bəl] *adj.* that can be or be done; able to happen: **The highest *possible* score on a test is 100 percent, which means you answered every question correctly.** [25]

praise [prāz] *v.* to say nice things about someone or something: **Her parents *praise* her when she gets good grades in school.** [30]

pre•his•tor•ic [prē´his•tôr´ik] *adj.* in the time before written records of history were kept: **No one knows exactly when people first came to the Americas, because it happened in *prehistoric* times.** [19]

pre•paid [prē´pād´] *adj.* paid in advance: **We got into the game for free because my dad's friend had left some *prepaid* tickets for us at the gate.** [19]

pre•serve [pri•zûrv´] *v.* to keep in good condition: **Foods such as corn, peas, or beans can be frozen or packed in cans to *preserve* them.** *syn.* maintain [13]

pret•ty [prit´ē] *adj.* **prettier, prettiest.** very nice to look at; pleasing to the eyes: **I think the green dress is *prettier* than the red one, but I'm going to buy the blue dress because it's the *prettiest* of them all.** [16]

prey [prā] *n.* an animal that is hunted by another animal for food: **A young deer might be the *prey* of a wolf.** [10]

a	add	ō	open	th	thin
ā	ace	ô	order	th	this
â(r)	care	oi	oil	zh	vision
ä	palm	o͝o	took		
e	end	o͞o	pool	ə	a in about
ē	equal	ou	out		e in listen
i	it	u	up		i in pencil
ī	ice	û(r)	burn		o in melon
o	odd	yo͞o	use		u in circus

prop•er•ty [prop´ər•tē] *n.* **properties.** **1.** anything that is owned by someone: **That book is her** *property,* **and you should ask to borrow it from her if you want to read it. 2.** a piece of land that someone owns: **The Smiths are planning to build a summer home on their** *property* **by the lake.** [16]

pub•lic [pub´lik] *adj.* belonging to or open to everyone: **Some of the** *public* **tennis courts have lights so that you can play at night.** [29]

pu•pil [py$\overline{oo}$´pəl] *n.* **1.** someone who goes to school; a student: **The** *pupil* **raised her hand to answer the question. 2.** the dark, central part of the eye that becomes larger or smaller so that a certain amount of light can enter: **The** *pupil* **looks like a black hole in the center of the eye.** [32]

pup•pet [pup´it] *n.* a small figure of a person or an animal that is moved by the hand or by wires or strings: *Pinocchio* **is the story of a** *puppet* **who comes to life and has many adventures.** [29]

pure [py$\overline{oo}$r] *adj.* not mixed with any other substance: *pure* **water, a sweater made of** *pure* **wool.** [13]

qual•i•fy [kwol´ə•fī´] *v.* **qualified, qualifying.** to meet certain standards in order to do something: **The team that wins this semifinal game will** *qualify* **for the finals.** [20]

qual•i•ty [kwol´ə•tē] *n.* **qualities.** a person's special features or characteristics: **Two** *qualities* **that Jason has are honesty and intelligence.** *syn.* trait [3]

quite [kwīt] *adv.* very much so; really: **The sign made it** *quite* **clear that no dogs were allowed on the beach.** [3]

rab•bit [rab´it] *n.* a small, furry animal with long ears and a short tail: **The** *rabbit* **hopped to the garden, looking for food.** [29]

rac•coon [ra•k$\overline{oo}$n´] *n.* a small animal that has brownish-gray fur, black markings on the face, a thick body, and a bushy, ringed tail: **The** *raccoon* **lives both on the ground and in trees.** [8] ◆

◆ **Raccoon** was a word that the English settlers made up when they first came to America. The raccoon was not known in Europe, so they used the Native American word for this animal.

---

ra•di•ance [rā´dē•əns] *n.* rays of light or heat: **the** *radiance* **of the sun on a clear day.** [2]

ran•sack [ran´sak´] *v.* **ransacked, ransacking.** to search a place in a fast, rough way, looking for something valuable to take: **The thief** *ransacked* **the house, trying to find money or jewelry.** [21]

re•al•ize [rē´ə•līz´] *v.* to come to know; become aware of: **Joan was daydreaming on the bus and didn't** *realize* **she had gone past her stop.** [2]

re•ceive [ri•sēv´] *v.* **received, receiving.** to come to have; get: **Aunt Beth said she sent me a birthday present more than two weeks ago, but I still have not** *received* **the package.** [12]

reel [rēl] *n.* a device that is used to wind film, tape, a fishing line, or the like: **a** *reel* **of motion-picture film.** [29]

re•gion [rē´jən] *n.* a certain part of the earth: **Camels are found in desert** *regions* **of Africa and Asia.** *syn.* area [7]

re•ly [ri•lī´] *v.* **relied, relying.** to depend on; trust: **When Claire was ill, she** *relied* **on Jeff to choose a good book for her.** [16]

re•mem•ber [ri•mem´bər] *v.* to think of again; bring back to mind: **Our dog is really big now, but I can** *remember* **when he was a tiny puppy.** [24]

re•port [ri•pôrt´] *n.* a statement that tells facts about something: **Annie is working on a** *report* **about tigers for her science class.** —*v.* to make such a statement: **Newspapers** *report* **on the news of the day.** [10]

res•er•va•tion [rez´ər•vā´shən] *n.* an area of land set aside for a special purpose: **That Native American tribe once had to live on a** *reservation* **set aside by the United States government.** [26]

re•turn [ri•tûrn´] *v.* to go back or come back: **We are going to drive north on Route 20 and then** *return* **home on the same road.** [13]

rib•bon [rib´ən] *n.* a long, narrow strip of cloth used to tie or trim something: **She used a blue** *ribbon* **to tie back her hair.** [25]

roam [rōm] *v.* to move around with no set route or purpose: **They let their dog run loose, and it just** *roams* **around the pasture all day.** [9]

rob•ber [rob´ər] *n.* a person who steals something: **The** *robber* **stole thousands of dollars from the safe.** [30]

route [r$\overline{oo}$t *or* rout] *n.* a way to travel from one place to another: **You should take Highway 9; that's the straightest** *route* **from here to the city.** [8]

roy•al [roi´əl] *adj.* having to do with a king or queen: **Prince Charles is a member of the** *royal* **family of Great Britain.** [14]

sad·ness   [sad´nis] *n.* a feeling of being sad; feeling bad: **He felt *sadness* when his best friend moved away to another town.** *syn.* sorrow [28]

scared   [skârd] *adj.* frightened: **The rabbit was *scared* when it saw us, and it ran off into the bushes.** *syn.* alarmed [15]

scent   [sent] *n.* something sensed by the nose; a smell: **It was a beautiful spring day, and the *scent* of flowers filled the air.** [9]

sci·ence   [sī´əns] *n.* the careful study of the world around us to learn the facts about it: **Botany is a field of *science* in which plant life is studied.** [7]

search   [sûrch] *v.* **searched, searching.** to look for something in a careful way; try to find something: **I *searched* the whole house and finally found my missing watch under the living room couch.** [13]

se·cure   [si·kyŏor´] *adj.* in a safe place or position; not dangerous: **Be careful on that ladder; it doesn't look very *secure*.** [13]

sel·dom   [sel´dəm] *adv.* not often: **Joanna is a very serious child; she *seldom* smiles.** *syn.* rarely [29]

send   [send] *v.* **sent, sending.** to cause to go to another place: **Drew *sent* a letter to his aunt.** [9]

sev·er·al   [sev´rəl *or* sev´ə·rəl] *adj.* more than one or two, but not many: There are *several* **different roads you can take to our school from here.** [25]

share   [shâr] *v.* to have or use a thing with another or others: **Melissa has her own bedroom, but her two brothers *share* a room.** [10]

shelf   [shelf] *n.* **shelves.** a long, flat board in a closet or cabinet to put things on: **Mrs. Doyle keeps her books on the *shelves* behind her desk.** [23]

short·stop   [shôrt´stop´] *n.* a baseball player whose position is between second and third base: **The *shortstop* often has to field ground balls hit to the left side of the infield.** [31]

shriek   [shrēk] *n.* a loud, high sound: **The *shriek-ing* of the birds was too loud to talk over.** *syn.* screaming [28]

shriv·eled   [shriv´əld] *adj.* shrunken and wrinkled from dryness or age: **The plants had not had any water, and their leaves were all *shriveled* up.** [21]

shut   [shut] *v.* **shut, shutting.** to move something in order to close an opening or passageway:

Please *shut* that door; it's letting in too much cold air. [4]

side·walk   [sīd´wôk´] *n.* an area to walk along the side of a road: **a concrete *sidewalk*.** [18]

si·es·ta   [sē·es´tə] *n.* a Spanish word for a nap in the afternoon: **People in Spain often take a *siesta* after lunch in the hot summer months.** [32]

sig·nal   [sig´nəl] *n.* something that gives a sign, message, or warning: **A fire engine uses flashing lights and a siren as a *signal* to cars to get out of the way.** —*v.* to make something known in this way: **In the days before radio, ships at sea used flags to *signal* to each other.** [30]

si·lence   [sī´ləns] *n.* the absence of sound; being silent: **The loud ringing of the alarm by the bed broke the early morning *silence*.** [32]

si·lent   [sī´lənt] *adj.* making no sound; completely quiet: **It was the middle of the night, and with everyone asleep the house was *silent*.** [31]

sil·ver   [sil´vər] *n.* a soft, white metal that is very valuable: **Jewelry and coins are often made of *silver*.** —*adj.* having the color of silver: **The *silver* dime sparkled in the sunlight.** [29]

since   [sins] *prep., adv.* during the time from then to now: **We've lived here *since* I was in first grade.** —*conj.* for that reason: ***Since* it is a holiday, our school is closed today.** *syn.* because [7]

sing   [sing] *v.* **sang, singing.** to use the voice to make musical sounds: **When she's in the car alone, she likes to *sing* along with the music from the radio.** [3]

sis·ter   [sis´tər] *n.* a female child who has the same parents as another: **I borrowed my *sister's* jacket because it's warmer than mine.** [21]

sixth   [siksth] *adj.* next after the fifth. [3]

skate   [skāt] *v.* **skated, skating.** to glide or move by means of ice skates or roller skates: **Lucy and Art are *skating* at the roller rink.** [15]

sleep   [slēp] *v.* **slept, sleeping.** to be in a state of rest; not be awake: **I *slept* for eight hours last night.** [2]

smell   [smel] *v.* to sense something with the nose: **to *smell* smoke, to *smell* dinner cooking.** [2]

a	add	ō	open	th	thin
ā	ace	ô	order	th	this
â(r)	care	oi	oil	zh	vision
ä	palm	ŏŏ	took		
e	end	ōō	pool	ə	a in about
ē	equal	ou	out		e in listen
i	it	u	up		i in pencil
ī	ice	û(r)	burn		o in melon
o	odd	yōō	use		u in circus

smoke·stack [smōk´stak´] *n.* a large chimney through which smoke escapes from a furnace or engine: **The ocean liner had three** *smokestacks.* [25]

smokestack

smooth [smo͞oth] *adj.* not rough or uneven: **Gina puts lotion on her hands to keep them** *smooth.* —*v.* to make smooth: **Pull the sheet tight, and** *smooth* **out the wrinkles.** [8]

sock [sok] *n.* a covering for the foot, worn under shoes: **The uniform for their soccer team is white shirts, red shorts, and red** *socks.* [6]

so·fa [sō´fə] *n.* a long piece of furniture to sit on: **We have a** *sofa* **in our living room.** [32]

so·lar [sō´lər] *adj.* having to do with the sun: **The** *solar* **shield on our roof collects heat from the sun.** [31]

solve [solv] *v.* to find out the answer or facts: **to** *solve* **a math problem, to** *solve* **a crime.** [6]

some·bod·y [sum´bud´ē *or* sum´bod´ē] *pron.* some person: **I don't know who it was, but** *somebody* **forgot to turn off the television.** [18]

some·how [sum´hou´] *adv.* in some way: **The cat** *somehow* **got up on top of my bookcase and went to sleep there.** [26]

south [south] *adj.* to or in the direction opposite of north: **Florida is** *south* **of Georgia.** [14]

space [spās] *n.* **1.** any area that has certain limits: **the** *space* **between lines in writing, a parking** *space* **for a car. 2.** the vast area beyond the earth that makes up the universe: **With this telescope, scientists can see far out into** *space.* [1]

speak [spēk] *v.* **spoke, speaking.** to use the voice to say words: **You'll have to** *speak* **louder because I can't quite hear you.** *syn.* talk [2]

spe·cial [spesh´əl] *adj.* not like others; unusual in some way: **The day my baby sister was born was a** *special* **day for our family that I remember very well.** [25]

spot [spot] *v.* **spotted, spotting.** picked out or recognized: **Jerry** *spotted* **his friends in the crowd.** —*adj.* having spots, marks, or stains: **Dalmatians are white dogs** *spotted* **with black.** [15]

spring [spring] *n.* **1.** the season that comes between winter and summer: **In** *spring,* **all the plants begin to grow again. 2.** a metal coil that goes back to its original shape after being pushed or pulled: **the** *springs* **of a car seat, the** *springs* **of a mattress.** —*v.* to move up into the air; jump: **A kangaroo can** *spring* **high off the ground.** [3]

spy [spī] *v.* **spied, spying. 1.** to watch in a secret way: **In the Revolutionary War, Nathan Hale** *spied* **on the British for the American army. 2.** to see suddenly and quickly: **Sam** *spied* **a deer running across the field.** [16]

squir·rel [skwûr´əl] *n.* a small furry animal with sharp teeth and a bushy tail: **A** *squirrel* **lives in the trees and feeds mostly on nuts.** [30]

stairs [stārz] *n.* a series of steps used for going from one level to another: **For exercise I walk up the** *stairs* **instead of taking the elevator.** [10]

stam·pede [stam·pēd´] *n.* a sudden, wild movement of animals or people in a group: **Thunder sent the frightened cattle into a** *stampede.* [18]

stand [stand] *v.* **stood, standing.** to move to or remain on one's feet: **The principal asked that each student** *stand* **when his or her name was called.** [1]

star [stär] *n.* **1.** a large object in space, similar to the sun, that appears in the night sky as a bright point of light: **A** *star* **is actually a huge ball of glowing gas. 2.** a figure that looks something like this, with points that go out from the center: **The flag of the United States has a** *star* **for each state. 3.** a person who plays an important part in a movie or play: **James Stewart was the** *star* **of the film** *It's a Wonderful Life.* [10]

star·tling [stär´tling] *adj.* causing sudden surprise: **The noisy blast of the horn was** *startling.* [16]

state [stāt] *n.* **1.** one of the parts that make up a country: **The United States is a nation made up of 50 different** *states.* **2.** the way something or someone is: **a person who is in a** *state* **of happiness.** *syn.* condition —*v.* to say in words: **to** *state* **the reasons for doing something.** *syn.* express [1]

stay [stā] *v.* to keep on in the same place or condition: **Remember to** *stay* **on the base until the pitcher throws the ball. She wore a raincoat so that her clothes would** *stay* **dry.** *syn.* remain [1]

step [step] *n.* the movement made in walking: **I almost have to run to keep up with Dad because he takes such big** *steps.* —*v.* **stepped, stepping.** to move by walking: **Cassie** *stepped* **very carefully over the broken glass.** [2, 15]

stew [sto͞o] *n.* a food made by cooking pieces of meat and vegetables very slowly in a thick liquid: **Beef** *stew* **is a good winter-time meal.** [4]

S

stick [stik] *v.* **stuck, sticking.** to catch or fasten in one place: **Our car was *stuck* in the snow, and we all had to push it to get it moving again.** [4]

stock [stok] *n.* things kept on hand for sale in a store: **His job at the store is to put *stock* on the shelves.** —*v.* to keep for sale in a store: **Does the music store also *stock* videotapes?** [6]

sto•ry [stôr´ē] *n.* **stories.** a telling of something that happens: *Cinderella* **is the *story* of a poor girl who marries a handsome prince.** [10]

street [strēt] *n.* a public road in a city or town, usually having sidewalks and buildings on either side: **Look both ways before you cross the *street*.** [2]

strike [strīk] *n.* in baseball, a pitch that goes over home plate and is not hit onto the field by the batter: **It takes three *strikes* to make an out.** [31]

stu•dent [stōod´ənt] *n.* a person who goes to a school, college, or the like: **My sister is a *student* at the University of Michigan.** [8]

stuff [stuf] *v.* to fill tightly; fill up: **Don't try to *stuff* all your clothes into that one small bag.** —*n.* any kind of material or substance: **What is that black *stuff* that's all over the rug?** [4]

stunned [stund] *adj.* very shocked or surprised: **She was so *stunned* to learn she had won the contest that she couldn't say a word.** [21] ♦

♦ **Stunned** is related to the word *thunder.* The idea is that a person would be stunned by suddenly hearing a loud crash of thunder.

---

sub•ject [sub´jikt] *n.* **1.** something that is talked or written about: **I wanted to ask Danny how his team lost the game, but I was afraid to bring up the *subject*. 2.** something that is studied in school: **History is her favorite *subject*. 3.** a person who is loyal to a ruler: **The *subject* told the king what had happened in the kingdom.** [30]

sud•den [sud´ən] *adj.* happening very quickly and without being expected: **Just as we sat down for the picnic, there was a *sudden* rainstorm and we all got soaked.** [29]

sum•mer [sum´ər] *n.* the season that comes between spring and fall: **In Florida, *summer* is the hottest time of the year.** [29]

sup•ply [sə•plī´] *n.* an amount of something that can be used: **We always keep a *supply* of candles on hand in case our electric lights go out in a storm.** —*v.* **supplied, supplying.** to give something that is needed or wanted: **The softball league *supplied* the players with uniforms.** *syn.* furnish [16, 20]

sur•vive [sûr•vīv´] *v.* to stay alive. [10]

swim [swim] *v.* **swam, swimming.** to move through the water, as a fish does: **She *swam* from one end of the pool to the other.** —*n.* the act or sport of going through the water by moving parts of the body: **As soon as the weather gets a little warmer we can go *swimming* in the ocean.** [1, 15]

swing [swing] *v.* **swung, swinging.** to move back and forth in a curve or circle: **The monkey *swung* from one tree limb to another as it moved through the forest.** [4]

teach•er [tē´chər] *n.* a person who helps others to learn; someone who instructs: **Next Friday there will be a *teachers'* meeting, and we have a day off.** [21]

team [tēm] *n.* a group of people who play together in a sport: **In our Little League, the *teams'* names are the same as those belonging to big-league teams.** [21]

tem•per [tem´pər] *n.* a state of mind, especially an angry state of mind: **He has quite a *temper* and will cry and pout if he doesn't get his way.** [30]

ten•ta•cle [ten´tə•kəl] *n.* a long, thin, flexible armlike structure that certain animals use for touching or for holding things: **The *tentacles* of a jellyfish can cause a painful sting.** [15]

tentacles of an octopus

a	add	ō	open	th	thin
ā	ace	ô	order	th	this
â(r)	care	oi	oil	zh	vision
ä	palm	ŏŏ	took		
e	end	ōō	pool	ə	a in about
ē	equal	ou	out		e in listen
i	it	u	up		i in pencil
ī	ice	û(r)	burn		o in melon
o	odd	yōō	use		u in circus

ter·ri·fied [ter´ə·fīd] *adj.* filled with fear; very much afraid: **When the earthquake hit, we were** *terrified* **that the building would fall down around us.** [16]

tes·ti·fy [tes´ti·fī] *v.* **testified, testifying.** to tell what one knows about a case in a court of law: **He is accused of stealing a car, and two witnesses will** *testify* **that they saw him driving the car later that same day.** [20]

thank [thangk] *v.* to say that one is grateful; give thanks: **Before you leave, be sure to** *thank* **Teri for inviting you to her party.** [1]

them·selves [ŧhem·selvz´] *pron.* their very selves; the ones they are: **In our house, Mom and Dad do the cooking** *themselves* **and don't expect us to help.** [26]

there·fore [ŧhâr´fôr´] *conj.* for that reason: **There is only a half day of school tomorrow;** *therefore,* **lunch will not be served in the cafeteria.** [10]

thief [thēf] *n.* **thieves.** a person who steals something: **I left my bicycle right here; some** *thief* **must have taken it.** [12]

thrive [thrīv] *v.* to grow very well; be healthy: **Crops such as corn** *thrive* **in the rich farmland of the American Midwest.** *syn.* flourish [13]

through [thrōō] *prep.* **1.** into one side of and out the other: **I looked** *through* **the tunnel and could see the light at the other end. 2.** by means of: **The magazine was sent to us** *through* **the mail.** —*adj.* finished; done: **If you're** *through* **using the phone, I want to make a call.** [8]

throw [thrō] *v.* **threw, throwing.** to send through the air, as with the hand: **Who** *threw* **the ball that broke that window?** [4]

ti·ger [tī´gər] *n.* a very large wild animal of the cat family that has thick black stripes on its orange-yellow fur. [31]

ti·ny [tī´nē] *adj.* very, very small: **I didn't know how the plant got holes in its leaves until I saw that there were** *tiny* **insects on the leaves.** [20]

tired [tīrd] *adj.* wanting to rest or sleep; not having the energy to work or do things: **Gary was very** *tired* **after running the five-mile race.** [15]

toe [tō] *n.* **toes.** one of the five parts at the end of the foot: **It feels good to dig your** *toes* **into the sand when you walk barefoot on the beach.** [6]

tooth [tōōth] *n.* **teeth.** one of the hard, white, bony parts in the mouth used for biting and chewing: **He lost a baby** *tooth* **while eating an apple. Lions have long, sharp** *teeth.* [8, 2]

torch [tôrch] *n.* **torches.** a burning or shining light at the end of stick or object that can be held in the hand: **The men lighted the cave with two fiery** *torches.* [25]

to·tem pole [tō´təm pōl´] *n.* a tall pole that is carved or painted with the images of animals and objects that have a special meaning: **The Native Americans of the Pacific Northwest carved family signs on their** *totem poles.* [26]

tra·di·tion [trə·dish´ən] *n.* a way of doing things that is passed down over time by the members of a group: **One of the** *traditions* **of baseball is that the home-team fans always stand up for the "seventh-inning stretch."** [26]

traf·fic [traf´ik] *n.* the moving of a number of cars or other vehicles along a certain route: **There was a lot of** *traffic* **going to the city today, and it took us twice as long as usual to get there.** [30]

trick [trik] *n.* **1.** an action that takes a special skill or talent: **Standing on my head is one** *trick* **that I have never been able to do. 2.** an action done to fool someone: **It was a mean** *trick* **to hide Cara's homework and make her think it was lost.** [3]

trip [trip] *n.* the act of traveling a distance from one place to another: **He was a little nervous because it was his first** *trip* **on an airplane.** *syn.* journey —*v.* to fall while walking or running: **Be careful that you don't** *trip* **over that wire.** [3]

trou·ble [trub´əl] *n.* something that causes a problem or difficulty: **She wants to sell that car right away because she has had nothing but** *trouble* **with it since she bought it.** [25]

trout [trout] *n.* a fish that is often found in rivers and lakes of North America. [29]

truck [truk] *n.* a motor vehicle used for moving large or heavy things: **The men loaded the bed into the back of the** *truck.*

truly [trōō´lē] *adv.* in fact; really; actually: **I'd like to be able to tell you his name, but I** *truly* **can't remember what it is.** [8]

truth [trōōth] *n.* that which is right or honest; what is according to the facts: **Marc told the** *truth* **when he said there was an eagle on the roof; I saw it myself.** [8]

tun·nel [tun´əl] *n.* a covered road or track that is underwater or below ground: **The "Chunnel" is a long** *tunnel* **that passes under the waters of the English Channel between England and France.** [30]

twi·light [twī´līt´] *n.* the lighting of the sky just as the sun goes down: **The boys headed home for dinner at** *twilight.* [9]

type [tīp] *n.* a group of items having certain things in common: **The orange is a** *type* **of fruit.** *syns.* kind, category —*v.* to write with a special machine that produces printed letters: **With a computer you** *type* **words on a keyboard, and they appear on the screen.** [3]

UFO [yōo´ef´ō´] *n.* an object that is seen moving across the sky but that cannot be identified as a plane or a natural event: **Some people claim to have seen a *UFO* and believe that they have actually seen a spacecraft from another planet.** [19] ♦

♦ **UFO** is a word that was formed by taking the first three letters of its longer name, <u>u</u>nidentified <u>f</u>lying <u>o</u>bject. This kind of word is called an *acronym*.

un•cer•tain [un•sûr´tən] *adj.* not certain; not sure; doubtful: **Millions of people get colds every winter, but doctors are still *uncertain* of a cure.** *syn.* doubtful [19]

un•e•ven [un•ē´vən] *adj.* not even; not smooth, level, or straight: **The old dirt road had not been fixed in many years, and it had a rough, *uneven* surface.** [19]

un•ex•pect•ed [un•ik•spek´tid] *adj.* not expected; coming as a surprise: **My uncle happened to be in town for a few hours and made an *unexpected* visit to our house.** [19]

u•nit•ed [yōo•nī´tid] *adj.* joined together; making up a unit: **the *United* States of America.** —*v.* to combine or join together: **The families *united* to form a new business.** [15]

un•lock [un•lok´] *v.* unlocked, unlocking. to open or unfasten a lock: **I used my house key and *unlocked* the door.** [19]

un•luck•y [un•luk´ē] *adj.* not lucky; having bad fortune: **Today is an *unlucky* day because I lost my wallet.** [19]

un•seen [un•sēn´] *adj.* not able to be seen; not in sight: **Wind is a powerful but *unseen* force.** [19]

un•tie [un•tī´] *v.* to loosen or undo something that is tied: **to *untie* your shoelaces before taking off your shoes.** [19]

un•u•su•al [un•yōo´zhōo•əl] *adj.* not usual; not normal or ordinary: **It's *unusual* to see snow in the month of May.** *syn.* uncommon [19]

use•less [yōos´lis] *adj.* having no use; not having a value or purpose: **She saves old magazines to read again, but old newspapers are *useless* to her and she throws them away.** [28]

voice [vois] *n.* the sound of speaking or singing that comes from the mouth: **The opera singer**

Marian Anderson is famous for her beautiful *voice*. [7]

vol•ca•no [vol•kā´nō] *n.* a cone-shaped mountain from which gases and lava erupt: **Molten lava flowed from the top of the *volcano*.** [18]

vote [vōt] *v.* to give one's choice or opinion in an election: **Every four years the people of the United States *vote* to choose someone to be President.** [6]

wal•let [wäl´it] *n.* a small folding case, often made of leather, used for carrying money: **My mother carries her driver's license, credit cards, and some family pictures in her *wallet*.** [29]

wa•ver [wā´vər] *v.* wavered, wavering. to move back and forth between two sides or ideas: **He couldn't decide which necktie to wear and kept *wavering* between the yellow one and the red one.** [1]

week•end [wēk´end´] *n.* the part of the week between Friday evening and Monday morning: **The beach is more crowded on Saturday and Sunday because many people have the *weekend* off.** [18]

weigh [wā] *v.* to find out how heavy something is; find out the weight of something: **Let's *weigh* this package on the scales.** [12]

weight [wāt] *n.* the measure of how heavy something is: **The butcher shop sells meat by the pound, so they have to find out the *weight* of each piece of meat to know how much to charge.** [12]

weird [wird] *adj.* strange and odd: **It was a *weird* story about a man who wakes up to find that he has turned into a plant.** *syn.* eerie [12]

wheel [wēl *or* hwēl] *n.* the round part that goes around to move a car, bicycle, or the like: **Jon's riding toy has one big *wheel* in front and two small ones in back.** [2]

whole [hōl] *adj.* all of something: **Dick didn't share his popcorn but ate the *whole* box by himself.** *syns.* complete, entire [9]

a	add	ō	open	th	thin
ā	ace	ô	order	th̶	this
â(r)	care	oi	oil	zh	vision
ä	palm	o͝o	took		
e	end	o͞o	pool	ə	a in about
ē	equal	ou	out		e in listen
i	it	u	up		i in pencil
ī	ice	û(r)	burn		o in melon
o	odd	yōo	use		u in circus

whom [hōōm] *pron.* a word used to ask about the person who was the object of some action: **The lawyer asked the witness, "*Whom* did you see leaving the bank that day?"** [8]

wild [wīld] *adj.* living or growing in a natural state; not under the control of humans: *wild* **flowers,** *wild* **animals such as the lion or tiger.** [3]

wil·der·ness [wil´dər·nis] *n.* an area not developed for people: **There are still many miles of** *wilderness* **in the state of Alaska.** [10, 28]

win [win] *v.* **won, winning.** to be first or in the lead in a game or competition: **When we were behind 5–0, I didn't think we had a chance of** *winning* **the game, but we came back to beat them.** [15]

wind·shield [wind´shēld´] *n.* a layer of protective glass or plastic at the front of a car, truck, or other motor vehicle: **Ted had to scrape the ice off the** *windshield* **this morning before he could drive the car.** [26]

wolf [wŏŏlf] *n.* **wolves.** a large wild animal of the dog family that hunts other animals: *Wolves* **live in family groups called** *packs*. [23]

wolf

wom·an [wŏŏm´ən] *n.* **women.** an adult female: **Chris Evert is one of the most famous players in the history of** *women's* **tennis.** [21]

won·der [wun´dər] *v.* to want to know about something; be curious: **Do you ever** *wonder* **what it would be like to travel in space?** *—n.* the state of being curious or amazed: **The children watched in** *wonder* **as the magician did his tricks.** [24]

won·der·ful [wun´dər·fəl] *adj.* impressive; outstanding: **From the top of the hill, we had a** *wonderful* **view across the valley to the mountains beyond.** [28]

wood·en [wŏŏd´ən] *adj.* made of wood: **Dad has a set of** *wooden* **toy soldiers that he played with when he was a child.** [8]

wool [wŏŏl] *n.* the soft hair that comes from the hair of sheep and other similar animals: **Sweaters, coats, hats, and other clothing are often made of** *wool*. [8]

work·er [wûr´kər] *n.* a person who does work: **The company has a lot more business now and plans to add ten new** *workers* **to its staff.** [13]

world [wûrld] *n.* the planet on which we live; the earth: **The blue whale is the largest animal in the** *world*. **Mt. Everest in Asia is the** *world's* **tallest mountain.** [13, 21]

worm [wûrm] *n.* a small, creeping animal that has a soft body and no legs: **I found a** *worm* **in our garden when I was digging a hole.** [13]

worst [wûrst] *adj.* being the most unpleasant or poorest result: **A mark of 100 percent is the best score you can get on a test; 0 percent is the** *worst* **score.** [13]

wound [wōōnd] *v.* **wounded, wounding.** to hurt or injure: **The bird** *wounded* **its wing when it fell out of the nest.** [9]

year [yēr] *n.* a period of time that is made up of 365 days (or in a leap year, 366 days), beginning on January 1 and ending on December 31: **The earth goes completely around the sun once during a period of one** *year*. [23]

yoke [yōk] *v.* **yoked, yoking.** to join together or attach things to something else by means of a wooden frame: **Many pioneers traveled west in covered wagons, pulled by two oxen that were** *yoked* **together.** [24]

yours [yôrz *or* yŏŏrz] *pron.* belonging to *you*; your own: **This pencil is mine, so that one must be** *yours*. [10]

The Writing Process

In writing, you can use a plan called the *writing process* to help you think of ideas and then write about them. These are the stages of the writing process.

The writing process helps you move back and forth through stages of your writing.

PREWRITING

Identify your task, audience, and purpose. Then choose a topic. Gather and organize information about the topic.

DRAFTING

Put your ideas in writing. Don't worry about making mistakes. You can fix them later.

RESPONDING AND REVISING

Reread your writing to see if it meets your purpose. Meet with a partner or a group to discuss and revise it.

PROOFREADING

Correct spelling, grammar, usage, mechanics, and capitalization errors.

PUBLISHING

Share your writing. Decide how you want to publish your work.

Tips for Using the Writing Process

. . . .

Here are some tips to help you use the stages of the writing process.

Prewriting

Sometimes you might find it difficult to think of a topic. Ideas for topics can come from many places: something you already know or would like to know more about, something you've read, or something that has happened to you.

You can organize your ideas in several ways. You might use a list, an outline, a story map, a web, or a drawing.

Drafting

When you put your ideas on paper, use your organizer to maintain the correct order. If you make a mistake, keep going. You can go back to it later.

Remember that when you finish each stage you can return to a previous stage or go on to the next stage.

Responding and Revising

When you read your own or someone else's writing, you might look for some of these things: a good beginning and ending, clear words, and details that relate to the topic.

When someone makes suggestions about your writing, you can decide whether or not to make the changes.

I'm not happy with what I've written, so I'm going to begin again.

Proofreading

When you have finished making changes, you are ready to fix your mistakes. Use editor's marks to mark mistakes and changes. Use the Proofreading Checklist to help you.

I'd better circle this word. I'll check the spelling in a dictionary when I finish proofreading.

Proofreading Checklist

☑ Circle any words you are not sure you have spelled correctly. Look them up in a dictionary, or ask someone who knows how to spell them.

☑ Look for words you have misspelled before. Add them to your Spelling Log.

☑ If you are unsure of how to spell a word, try saying the word slowly. Listen to every syllable. Have you written all the syllables?

☑ Make sure you have indented each paragraph.

☑ Check your capitalization and punctuation.

☑ Do you want to take something out or add something?

Publishing

Here are some ideas you can use to publish your work.

- Read it aloud.
- Turn it into a play or a Readers Theatre.
- Print it on the computer.
- Make an audiotape or a videotape.
- Illustrate your story, and show the pictures as your audience listens to you read.

Spelling Strategies

Welcome to our classroom! Come on in, and we'll show you some of our favorite spelling strategies!

Here's a tip that helps me spell a word. I say the word. Then I picture the way it is spelled. Then I write it!

When I'm learning how to spell a word, the Study Steps to Learn a Word are a big help. See pages 8 and 9.

shout?

show?

I think of ways to spell the vowel sound in a word. Then I try different spellings until the word looks right.

When I don't know how to spell a word, sometimes I just take my best guess! Then I check it.

Sometimes I read the words backward. I start with the last word and end with the first word. It really helps me notice words I've misspelled! Then I proofread for meaning.

I proofread my work twice. First, I circle words I know are misspelled. Then I look for words I'm not sure of.

I look for homophones and make sure each word I've written makes sense.

When I'm writing a compound word, I think about how the two smaller words are spelled. That helps me!

Sometimes thinking of a rhyming word helps me figure out how to spell a word. I try to remember rules like making the right changes before adding -ed or -ing.

Drawing the shape of a word helps me remember how to spell it. This is the shape of the word *balanced*.

To help me remember how to spell *concentrate*, I remember that it has *cent* and *rate* in it.

I like to use silly sentences to help me remember a spelling. To spell *series*, I think of *Sally eats raisins in every sandwich.* The first letter of each word spells *series!*

Integrated Spelling

MY SPELLING LOG

What's a Spelling Log?

It's a special place where you can keep track of words that are important to you. Just look at what you'll find in your Spelling Log!

WORDS TO STUDY

pages 172–177

This is just the place for you to list words you need to study. There is a page for each unit of your spelling book.

Words to Explore

Every spelling lesson has Words to Explore. List them where you think they belong on special pages for . . .

Language...pages 178–179
Social Studies...pages 180–181
Math and Science...page 182
Art and Music...page 183

MY OWN WORD COLLECTION

pages 184–192

Be a word collector, and keep your collection here! Sort words you want to remember into fun categories you make up yourself!

EMERALD FOREST   Spelling Log • Harcourt Brace School Publishers

WORDS TO STUDY

UNIT 1

This page has a chalkboard for each lesson in Unit 1. On each one, list the words from that lesson that need your special attention. Those words will be easy to find when you're ready to study them.

Be sure to list the words you misspelled on the pretest. And it's a good idea to put in any other words from the lesson that you aren't sure you can spell correctly.

Lesson 1

Lesson 2

Lesson 3

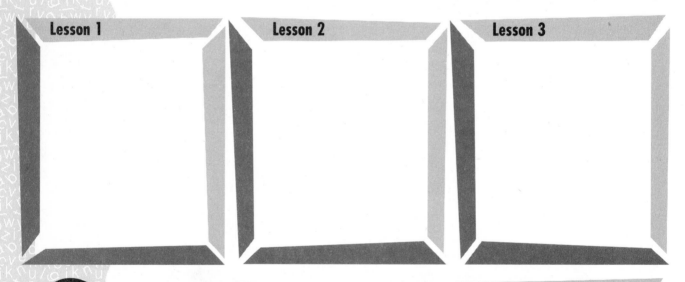

I'm going to use the study steps on pages 8 and 9 to help me learn these words!

Lesson 4

Words to Watch For

EMERALD FOREST Spelling Log • Harcourt Brace School Publishers

WORDS TO STUDY

UNIT 2

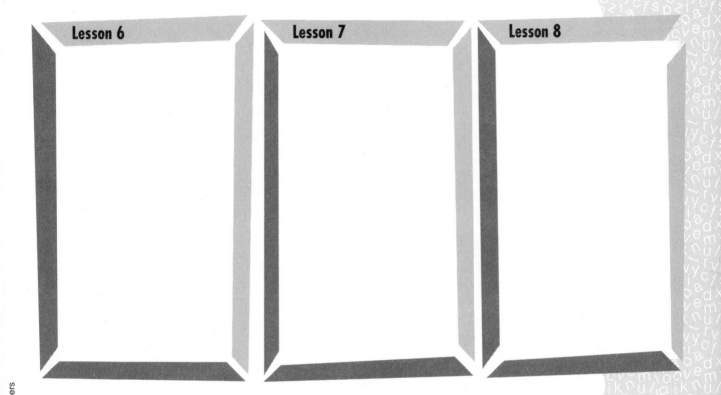

Lesson 6

Lesson 7

Lesson 8

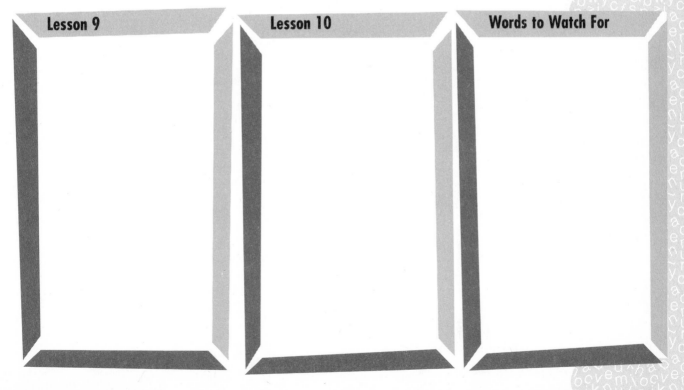

Lesson 9

Lesson 10

Words to Watch For

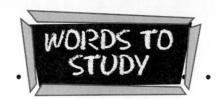

WORDS TO STUDY

UNIT 3

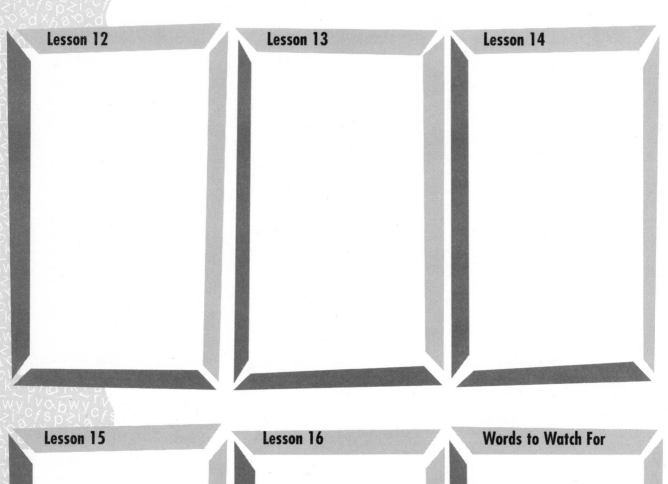

Lesson 12

Lesson 13

Lesson 14

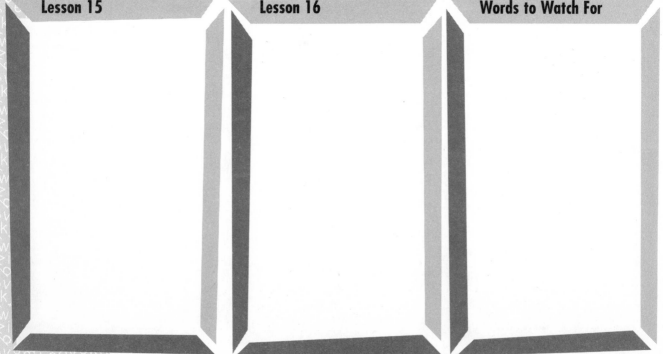

Lesson 15

Lesson 16

Words to Watch For

EMERALD FOREST Spelling Log • Harcourt Brace School Publishers

Integrated Spelling

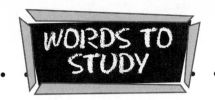

WORDS TO STUDY

UNIT 4

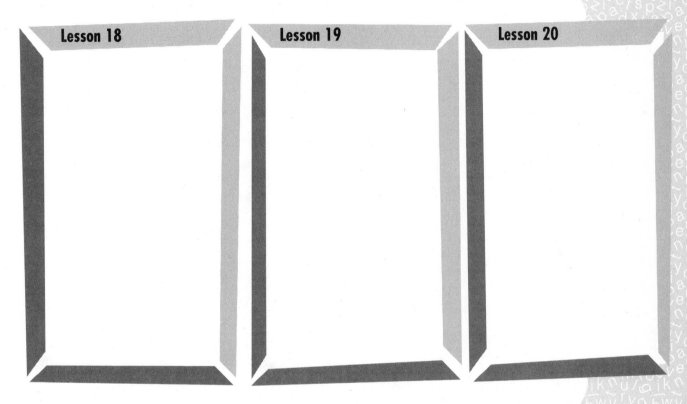

Lesson 18

Lesson 19

Lesson 20

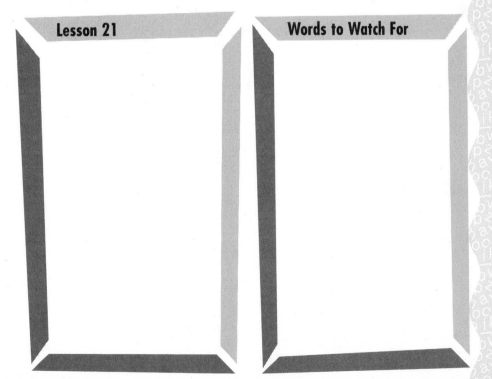

Lesson 21

Words to Watch For

EMERALD FOREST Spelling Log • Harcourt Brace School Publishers

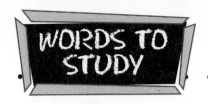

WORDS TO STUDY

UNIT 5

Lesson 23

Lesson 24

Lesson 25

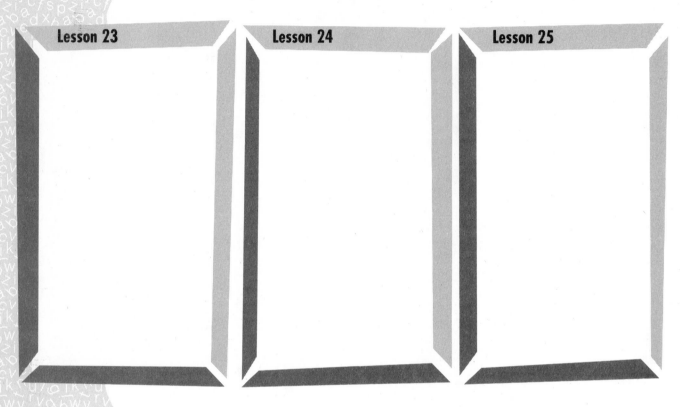

Lesson 26

Words to Watch For

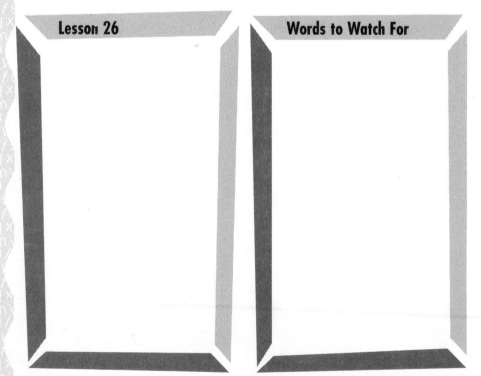

Integrated Spelling

WORDS TO STUDY

UNIT 6

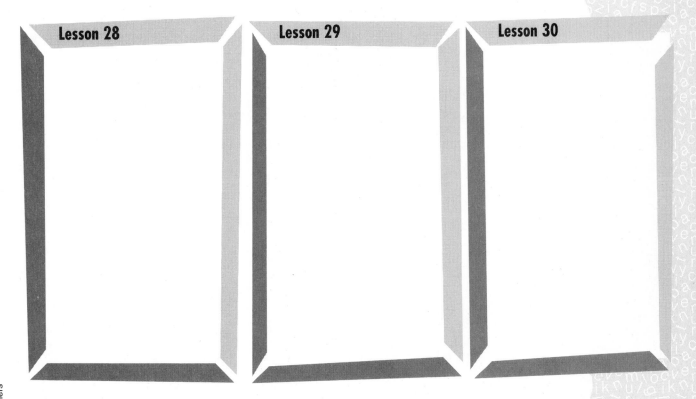

Lesson 28

Lesson 29

Lesson 30

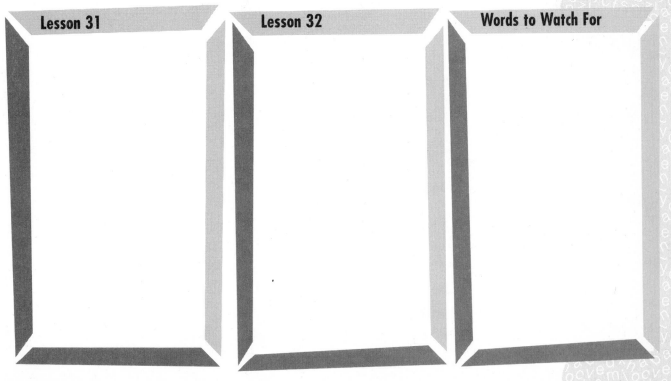

Lesson 31

Lesson 32

Words to Watch For

Words to Explore

Language

These pages are for listing Words to Explore. Group words that you think go together in a category. The clues in the margins may give you some ideas about ways to group them. Use ideas of your own, too!

Action Words

i before e words

Fancy Words

Funny Words

BIG Words

Delicious Words

VIVID Adjectives

Proper Nouns

Poetry Words

EMERALD FOREST Spelling Log • Harcourt Brace School Publishers

Words to Explore

Language

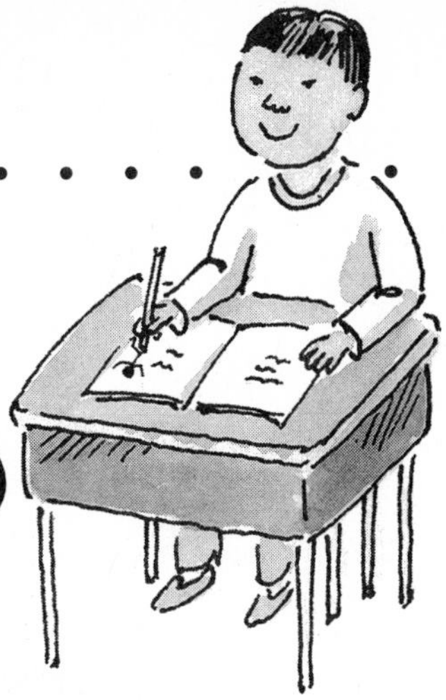

If you like, add a clue beside a word to help you remember it. The clue might be a picture, a sentence, a definition, or just a note. Here's what I'm going to add to help me remember what an acrobat is.

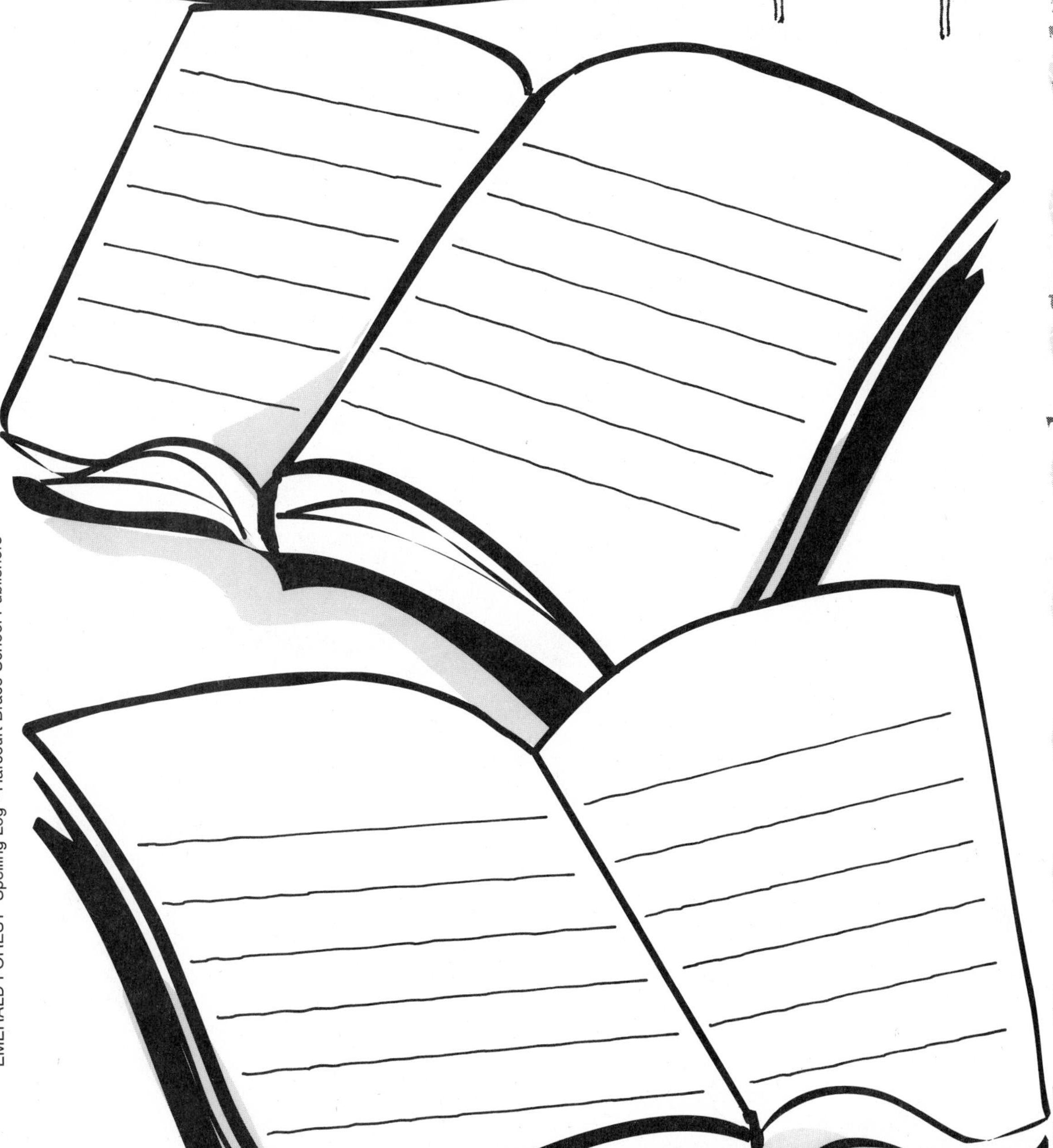

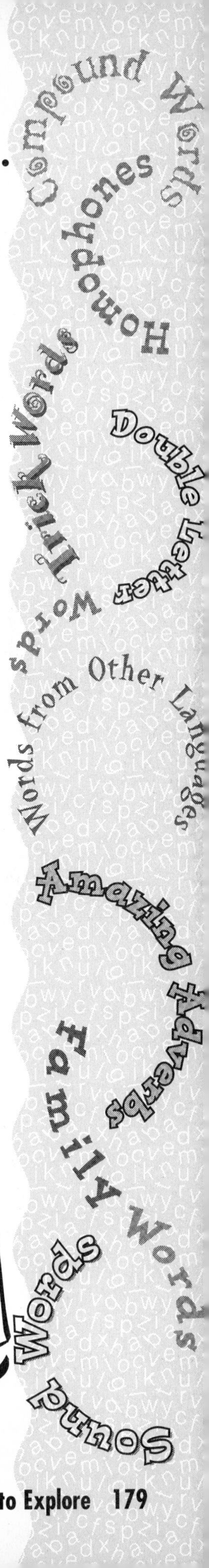
Compound Words
Homophones
Double Letter Words
Trick Words
Words from Other Languages
Amazing Adverbs
Family Words
Sound Words

EMERALD FOREST Spelling Log • Harcourt Brace School Publishers

Places

City Words

Map Words

Mountain Words

Money Words

Government Words

Transportation Words

Jungle Words

We learned about mountains and valleys in social studies. On these two pages, I'm going to list words that tell about types of land.

EMERALD FOREST Spelling Log • Harcourt Brace School Publishers

Integrated Spelling

Words
to Explore

Social Studies

Country Words

Desert Words

Communication Words

Occupations Words

Factory Words

Historical Words

Farm Words

River Words

Words to Explore

Math and Science

I'll put math and science words into groups on this page.

EMERALD FOREST Spelling Log • Harcourt Brace School Publishers

Integrated Spelling

Words
to Explore

Art and Music

This page is for art and music words!

Words
Musical Words
Color Words
Crafts
Names of Instruments
Painting Words
Art Supply Words
Rhythmic Words

EMERALD FOREST Spelling Log • Harcourt Brace School Publishers

My Own Word Collection

I collect baseball cards. Can I collect words, too?

Sure! When you read and listen, be on the lookout for words you want to remember. Group them into categories any way you like, and write them on these pages. Pretty soon you'll have a word collection of your very own!

Integrated Spelling

MY OWN WORD COLLECTION

Scary Words

Hard-to-Say Words

Pet Words

Celebration Words

Messy Words

Sports Words

Hard-to-Group Words

Sensory Words

Integrated Spelling

MY OWN WORD COLLECTION

I've learned lots of new words by adding them to my collection.

Unusual Words • Icy Words • New Words • Wet Words • Noisy Words • Outdoor Words • Awesome Words • Exciting Words!!!

EMERALD FOREST Spelling Log • Harcourt Brace School Publishers

Integrated Spelling

MY OWN WORD COLLECTION

The words in my collection help me say exactly what I mean!

Scary Words
Hard-to-Say Words
Pet Words
Celebration Words
Messy Words
Sports Words
Hard-to-Group Words
Sensory Words

Integrated Spelling